Bustamante
and
His Letters

Bustamante and His Letters

by Frank Hill

Published by: LMH Publishing Ltd.
Suite 10-11
Sagicor Industrial Park
7 Norman Road
Kingston C.S.O; Jamaica
Tel: 876-938-0005
Fax: 876-928-8036
Email: lmhbookpublishing@cwjamaica.com
Website: www.lmhpublishing.com

Printed in the USA   ISBN: 978-976-8202-72-7

Bustamante

and His Letters...

Contents

Chapter 1

The year was 1884. Half a century earlier the bitter struggle of the African slaves for freedom had been joined with the compelling need of an aggressive British industrial capitalism for free wage labour to produce, in one resolute flash, the Emancipation. But freedom is a delicate plant that has to be constantly nourished with tears and sweat and blood. So 21 years after Emancipation and 19 years before Bustamante was born, Paul Bogle and George William Gordon, now acclaimed as National Heroes, had to make their rebellion in Morant Bay. But it was remote enough in time for the memory of their bloody dash for freedom to grow dim and dull. Long enough to take a new look at the whole system of Crown Colony government that had followed the local abdication of representative government after Morant Bay. So the aging British Queen Victoria, widowed these past 23 years, was preparing Jamaica to take a mincing step forward on the road of slow return to the representative system.

Most of the political field was still fallow in spite of 1865. But the British conscience had been vaguely stirred to make sporadic efforts to correct some of the grosser imbalances in the social structure. Jamaica was still predominantly a big sugar plantation, with 72 sugar mills crisscrossing the island. But the banana had been imported from Guadeloupe, the French territory down in the eastern Caribbean. Its burgeoning cultivation was steadily becoming a promising inter-cropping to sugar cane; particularly to a new class of small farmers whose numbers were increasing on the hillsides and here and there on the flat lands of a few large (and profitless) estates cut up for settlements.

The nurturing of this small farmer class was a policy being deliberately pursued by the Crown Colony Governor, Sir John Peter ("Papa") Grant, to head off any repetition of the Morant Bay rebellion. The resistance to the surrender of the Constitution in 1865 had been muted; but the coloured middle class was expanding rapidly and when they made junction with the burgeoning class of freeholders, Grant knew that the movement to recover the old form of representative government would be well-nigh irresistible. In 1872, his last year as governor, he laid plans for a Jamaican University to train the administrators who would be called upon to share in the responsibility of governing Jamaica. He named it Queen's College of Jamaica, located it in King's House in the capital city of Spanish Town. Then he shifted the capital to Kingston, took over the Bishop's Lodge on the Hope Road in St. Andrew for the New King's House. Queen's College, empowered to award diplomas and degrees up to the level of the

Master's, was opened with a blare of trumpets in September 1873. After keeping its register open for a week, the college got three enrolments. Early the next year one more undergraduate was added. No other student came forward to increase the numbers for the second academic year and, with the death of the Principal, William Chadwick, at mid-year, this first enterprise in higher education was regretfully wound up before the new academic year started.

A railway line had been thrown down from the new Capital, Kingston, to the old Capital, Spanish Town, that promised further expansion northwards to the seaport town of Port Antonio, and a longer link bisecting the island to Montego Bay. The rugged Rio Cobre river had been caged just outside the old capital to provide a crude irrigation system for the St. Catherine plains. Even then a visionary eye was being cast over its hydro-electric potential. The first hesitant steps had been taken over forty years earlier to organise the slippery, individualistic merchant class into a Chamber of Commerce, but their natural tendency towards secretiveness was making the going tough. A cultivated British Governor, seeking to plant a rare species in a wild cultural jungle, had set up the Institute of Jamaica "for the encouragement of Literature, Science and Art". The colonial government's housekeeping budget for the year was under one million pounds. These imposts were collected from a population of 800,000 souls, only 14,000 of whom were eligible, under the income and property qualifications of the day, to vote. A political party was an unfamiliar phrase. A trade union was a conspiracy punishable by Law.

This was the world into which William Alexander Bustamante was born. But his surname wasn't Bustamante then; it was Clarke. And his mother abbreviated his first name and called him Willie. But his other relatives and close friends called him Aleck.

Hanover was a remote parish at the western bulge of the island. It was an area of large, sprawling farms, for the process of re-settling the estates had not yet penetrated this far. Way back into the century, before Emancipation, a comely St. Elizabeth girl, Elsie Hunter, married a thriving small farmer, Robert Clarke. They had one son whom they named Robert, though he was stuck with the pet name of Bobby. Then Robert Clarke died. Elsie, still fresh with youthfulness, married Alexander Shearer, a robust Irish farmer. This was a real catch for Elsie, for Shearer owned one of the largest estates in the parish - Blenheim - several hundred acres of sugar cane, timber and grasslands with its own great house that bore ample evidence of his wealth and respectability. The Shearers produced four girls who grew up on the spacious property along with their half-brother, Bobby Clarke. In due course Bobby took himself a wife. They had two children, both girls: Ida and Daisy. And when Bobby's wife died, he took himself another, Mary Wilson - a handsome dark-skinned girl from Lucea. Out of this second union came five children: Louise, Iris and Maud were the girls, Herbert and William Alexander were the boys.

Meantime, the four Shearer girls were blossoming into radiant womanhood. The eldest, Margaret Ann, went into the government service, became a Postmistress in Porus. There she was courted by an enterprising produce dealer named Thomas Manley who had a medium-sized farm in Manchester that he called Roxburgh. After the wedding, Thomas took Margaret Ann to Roxburgh, a rambling four-bedroom bungalow, with a high panelled, unceiled drawing room that made it palatial by the middle-class rural standards of those times. The first two children the Manleys produced were girls: Vera *(later Mrs. Ludlow Moody)*, and Muriel *(Dr. Muriel Manley)*; then came Norman, to whom they gave the middle name of Washington in admiration of the Father of American Independence, and finally Roy who was fated to die on a European battlefield in the early years of the first world war. When Norman Manley was nine years old, his father died; so the widow Manley packed up her two pairs of children and moved to Belmont, a cattle property in St. Catherine, where by careful, efficient management, she reared her offspring in sturdy comfort.

Back in Blenheim in Hanover, the third Shearer girl, Ellie, had married an English Anglican clergyman, Henry Swithinbank, who later took his wife and two children back to Kent in England. The Swithinbanks finally had nine children, the fifth of whom was Edna, later to become Mrs. Norman Manley. In the meantime, however, the remaining Shearers and their parents were having a difficult time. *"Old Man"* Shearer's eyesight was failing, throwing the burden of managing Blenheim more and more on Grandma Shearer. She found able assistance in her son, Bobby, who was promoted to be overseer. Bobby had been allowed to build a two-room cottage of timber from the property by his step-father. The cottage was some distance from the great house but sited on the property itself. All of Bobby's seven children by his two marriages had been born in this cottage. There had been three or four other children who failed to survive infancy. But with his new responsibility as Overseer, Bobby was allowed to bring his family to live in the great house; and in due course young Aleck striding through his lanky adolescence, was saddled with specific chores as the likely heir to the property. These included the breaking-in of the more spirited horses - a skill in which Aleck became expert. Eventually Grandpa Shearer's eyesight left him. After long, thoughtful consideration, Grandma turned over the management of Blenheim entirely to Bobby and took her blind husband to Belmont in St. Catherine, there to spend the rest of their days under the watchful eyes of daughter Margaret Ann Manley. With her blind husband, Grandma Shearer took along Aleck's eldest sister, Maud, who had earlier been adopted into her second family. So from about 1903 until 1911 when Margaret Ann Manley died, Belmont became a sort of second home for the Shearers and the Clarkes. In addition to Maud, Aleck's youngest sister, Iris, lived at Belmont for many years before migrating to New York where she became a nurse; and his third sister, Louise, was also a constant visitor and resident.

The young man Aleck Clarke joined his grandmother at Belmont in 1904. He came to be trained as an Overseer. The plan was that eventually he would return to Blenheim with higher skills in what was to be his life's work. The training period was to occupy one year. But during this time Aleck met a remarkable young man named David Mullings. They became firm friends. Mullings was employed at Belmont as a Coachman: he drove the Manleys and their relatives in the horse-drawn carriage, cared for the animals: performed the endless domestic chores that a Coachman - a kind of upper servant - should perform. But Mullings was no ordinary servant. He had a restless mental energy and an irresitible ambition to make his way in the world. He nurtured a clear-eyed vision that centred on Cuba: a promised haven of hope that stirred most Jamaican hearts to eager longing. Mullings talk to Aleck of his own hopes that grew little into plans. Aleck caught his infectious enthusiasm. Mullings encouraged his lanky, gangling friend: they were two of a kind: bold, adventuresome, and there seemingly was a whole new world waiting outside to pour fame and riches in the laps of those who were willing to dare. Why not both of them - together? Aleck wove his own dreams and struck a bargain. The two young men packed their few belongings and departed from Belmont for Cuba. The year was 1905. Bustamante, therefore, left Jamaica for the first time when he was 21. For the next 29 years a blank curtain was to descend on the activities abroad of Aleck Clarke. Facts were later to be blown up into fantasy and stretched into legend, most of it inspired by Aleck himself. But we can piece a fair picture together by sticking to the bare bones of the outline that came to be established.

Aleck did well enough in Cuba. He worked for a while as a special constable in the police force in Havana. Then he got a job with the tramway company which operated both in Cuba and in Panama. While in Cuba he was transferred to Panama and promoted to the rank of traffic inspector. In 1912 he returned to Jamaica for a brief visit; long enough, however, to get married. His bride was a Miss Sophie Plummer, one of the family of spinsters who lived in "Marie Villa" in Church Street in Downtown Kingston. The wedding was held in the modest bungalow on the high rise above the street. Then after a short honeymoon Aleck went back to Cuba - alone. And for the next ten years the history runs to earth. There is no one except himself who can say with any degree of accuracy just where he was or what he did in those years between the ages of 28 and 38. But this is the period into which he packed a number of conflicting stories - perhaps deliberately, in order to create the later legends. Mullings had gone to the United States where he became a qualified engineer and thereafter their paths did not cross. But the legend is worth noting: that he went from Cuba to Panama where he worked for a short while as a traffic inspector; that he shipped out from Panama under a captain who grew fond of him, adopted him, gave him his own name of Bustamante; that he wound up in Spain where he served in the army under General Primo de Rivera who later seized power and set up a military dictatorship with the acquiescence of King Alfonso XIII. In his later years Bustamante even displayed a certificate from a Spanish university showing him to have graduated with a degree in literature.

But the romantic, imaginative legend aside, the next glimpse Jamaica had of him was in 1922. He came on a flying visit from Cuba and remained only a few weeks. The visit was long enough, however, to show Aleck Clarke in the role of a Cuban "grandee" or gentleman.

When Bustamante left for Cuba on the third round in 1922, the gangling, gawky young man of ten years earlier, now sprouted an air of prosperity; he wore his clothes with meticulous care and with a general stylishness that showed how well he had absorbed the attitudes of a Cuban man of affairs.

In the meantime, however, his wife, Sophie, had died. Sophie's sister, Cassandra, had married a Kingston Land Surveyor, William B. Sangster, in 1910. The Sangsters made their home in St. Elizabeth where their son, Donald Burns Sangster, was born the next year and up to the time of his death in the middle twenties, William Sangster pursued his profession as a Surveyor in St.

Elizabeth.

The next glimpse of Aleck Clarke in Jamaica came in 1928, when he returned home, but this time with the intention of staying and establishing himself. In a determined effort he went into the dairy business. He put his boisterous energy singlehandedly into his enterprise. But he could not make a go of it and in 1929 he went back to Cuba. Two years later he returned home, this time with the idea that money could be made in bee-keeping. But he saw his mistake even more quickly than he had with dairying and the same year he was off again to Cuba. But by now Cuba had been displaced as his Promised Land. In its place loomed the United States. Aleck Clarke shipped out of Havana and when he turned up in New York, he was calling himself Alejandro Bustamanti, a cultivated white gentleman of Spanish birth.

In America Bustamanti had a varied career. At one time he was in Boston. There he gave shelter to his nephew, Donald Purcell, son of his sister, Louise, who had lived with the Manleys at Belmont while he attended school. Donald went to the famous Massachussetts Institute of Technology in Boston from which he graduated eventually to become a highly placed motor engineer in the research field. But it was New York that Bustamanti met a Canadian nurse, Mildred Edith Blanck, who became his second wife. The record of their marriage in New York's Bureau of Health lists him as *"Alejandro Bustamanti"* who is described as *"of Spanish origin"*. That was in 1932.

Among his various occupations in New York was that of hospital attendant at one of New York's better known private hospitals. In New York, too, Bustamanti may have speculated on Stock Exchange, and acquired a *"nest egg"*, but if this was so the exact amount must remain a mystery. Apparently, it was large enough for the migrant son, now turned 50, to consider heading back home — this time permanently.

And so in 1934, the native son came home — to be known from then onwards as Alexander Bustamante, and to start building his fame as a man of public affairs.

Chapter 2

The Jamaica to which Alexander Bustamante returned in 1934 was not noticeably different from the society he had first left 30 years earlier. But he was seeing it from a new angle. He had carried in his mind a picture of rural society of broad acres, open spaces, the spacious movement of its own measured way of living. He had understood this environment, though its sluggish pace, seemingly leading nowhere, had irked his bustling spirit. He had felt it a drag on his enterprising vision of *"going places and doing things"*. That was why he had broken out of what was almost a physical strait-jacket. That was why he had fled to Cuba — in the first instance; and that was what had propelled him onwards to the cities of America. But now he had seen all the places he wanted to see: he had acquired enough so that he could return home without being considered a failure and the achievement was enough. A man always wanted a place to call his own. This little island was home: and the achievement was enough to set him up in the life of a person of independent means. So he opened an office in Duke Street at the corner of Water Lane in down-town Kingston. His small, modestly furnished office had no nameplate outside its door. There was no need. The business he carried on inside was that of moneylender and his clients could be expected to seek him out. It was from this ringside seat in the heart of the island's capital that he could take a new, sharp look at the society into the public life of which he had decided to plunge with intelligent calculation.

What were the essential characteristics of Jamaican Society in terms of its economy? Jamaica was even more of a two-crop economy than he had imagined. If the British Governor, living in aloof isolation deep in the heart of fashionable, suburban St. Andrew, was king in a personal sense that everyone could understand, sugar was the crown prince. For the sugar industry was almost exclusively British owned and operated. It was the mainstay of the island's economy. True, in terms of British and international trade, it had fallen from the pinnacle of economic supremacy in the latter and opening decades of the 18th and 19th centuries respectively when on the basis of slave labour it had helped to make the fabulous fortunes on which the British industrial revolution was founded and expanded. But in 1934 it still represented a sufficiently substantial segment of capital investment, when added to those other segments in the rest of the West Indies (including British Guiana) to guarantee Britishers at home a sizeable reserve of cheap sucrose for their high tea to say nothing of the salaries paid to expatriate Englishmen who filled supervisory and managerial posts throughout the Caribbean. But a royal court, even if it is disguised as an economy, needs courtiers. The banana, the second crop, was the leading courtier. In its development during the past 70 years, its cultivation had given a firm base to the establishment of a rugged, peasant or small farmer class who had stabilised village life, building up traditions of a folk culture, deeply conservative, around religion, the family (concubinage), the superiority of the white race and the doctrine of British Judicial infallibility.

So the Jamaican economy, predominantly agricultural, was divided between sugar for the large planters, nearly all direct descendants of the liberated slaves of a hundred years earlier, and at least in economic terms, only slightly removed from the conditions of their forebears. The products of these two main crops were exported to British ports to feed the metropolitan economy. These two crops were about the only sources of wealth that were created within the island's boundaries. The proceeds of their sale paid for the imported food, clothing and building materials on which the island's people subsisted. For there was no native industry worth the name. This was deliberate imperial policy. The reality was disclosed when the colonial office, speaking through the British Governor, rebuffed local efforts to set up paper and cement factories, both of which would have cut into imports from Britain thereby setting dangerous precedents (from the imperial point of view) for the rest of the West Indies to follow. So industrialisation was a dangerous, alien word. The island's economy was set on a pre-determined course, ordained (by God, some white missionaries said) to be a producer of raw materials for British industrial factories and consumers of the manufactured products of these factories, 5,000 miles away. And if that made the majority of Jamaicans *"hewers of wood and drawers of water"*, well, somebody had to do the donkey work: the slaves up to a century earlier, their direct descendants in the post-Emancipation period.

But if industrialisation was a dirty word, *"development"* was the fashionable word that had enlivened governors' despatches to London for a long time. Three years before Bustamante was born, the governor, Anthony Musgrave, had borrowed £14,860 to throw bridges across some of the dangerous rivers on the north coast of Portland, then burgeoning into prosperous banana production. In the last decade of the waning century, another governor, Henry

Norman, negotiated two loans, one of £105,140 and a supplementary loan of £43,740 for further river-bridging to serve both road traffic and the projected railway extension to Port Antonio. Norman's successor, Henry Blake, took the borrowing splurge even further: he raised £100,000 for new interior main roads and bridges, £140,000 to reconstruct parochial roads, £100,000 for prisons, the lunatic asylum and the Kingston Public Hospital, and £44,250 for hill roads. Blake also borrowed money to build hotels to encourage the tourist trade. These loan funds were not expended on *"development projects"* as we understand the phrase in its modern sense. They were used to develop an infra-structure that could help to raise the island's backward public services closer to the level demanded by modern standards of civilisation. But there was no carefully thought out philosophy behind loan efforts until 1931 when the governor, Edward Stubbs, set up a *"Development Committee"* under his own chairmanship and explained to the Legislative Council in the debate on its first official report:

"Development did not mean the mere development of bananas and other produce; they must also include in it the mental, moral and spiritual development to be derived from schools, post-offices and civilisation, and even police stations and court houses. The Committee had taken it to be the desire of the Council that they should take into consideration and recommend anything that they considered for the good of the country, for its development in the sense of these improvements and civilisation, and the manner in which they should be financed".

But while there was a careful calculation that loan funds would be expended only on projects that were likely to be reproductive, if only indirectly and in the long term, there was never any thought of allowing even an elementary manufacturing complex to be established. A Native Industry law had been passed in 1933 under which a match factory had been established, making Beacon matches in competition with the Vulcan brand imported from Sweden. But no British interest had been at stake, so the match factory set no precedent. The Government's revenues retained the pattern that they had for generations: they came from customs and excise duties principally; direct taxation, mainly land taxes, was minimal. So, in simple, uncomplicated terms, the Jamaican economy was an import-export economy: the people lived on imports of nearly all their consumer necessities plus the few luxuries that the tiny minority of the affluent could afford, and the country paid for these imports with the proceeds of its sugar, bananas and rum that were sold in the British market.

The political system reflected the structure of the economy and of the vested interests of the realm. The minor variation in straight Crown Colony rule that had been effected the year that Bustamante was born — nine representatives elected on a limited franchise as a minority in an otherwise wholly nominated Legislative Council — had been improved in 1895 when the number of elected representatives was increased to 14, but the governor's nominees remained in the majority. There had been an attempt at further improvement in 1922. The colonial office proposed that the Legislative Council should be re-vamped to give the 14 elected representatives a majority of four over the 10 officials nominated by the governor, with the four unofficial nominated members being always free to vote according to their personal views, but with the governor retaining his reserve power to decide an issue contrary to a majority vote of the council is a matter declared by him to be of paramount public importance. The Colonial Office also proposed the creation of an Executive Committee, in addition to the Privy Council, which would include some elected members, this Committee to be the body to advise the governor and to deal with such matters, financial or otherwise, as he might wish to bring before it.

These proposals were discussed in the Legislative Council in 1926. But the elected members, lacking any sort of cohesion, were hopelessly divided and the Council rejected the proposals. So the British Governor remained in absolute charge of the island colony, with reserve powers that made him, with his Privy Council advisers, judge, jury and executioner. His Legislative Council of 28 members (only one-half of whom were elected) over which he presided with his ruling casting vote, was merely a chamber of grievance, in which the governor and his slate of nominees took all the initiatives of legislation and felicitous resolutions, while the elected members were confined to negative, destructive criticism. They had a small, delaying power: if nine of the fourteen voted against a financial measure, the motion would be defeated; but the governor, presiding, could declare the measure a matter of *"paramount importance"* and the governor's wishes would prevail. But even the democratic facade of national elections every five years could not hide the narrow representative base. The voting franchise was based on the ownership of property that yielded the owner a direct income of at least £150 a year, or an income otherwise of £300 a year, or the payment of direct taxes, land income of property, of not less than 10/- a year. This last named class of voters — the ten-shilling voter — might have ensured a large proportion — even a majority — of *"small men"* on the voters' rolls; but the system required the voter to apply for registration with proof (his tax receipts) of his qualification before he could get on the list. This proved, for the most part, to be too onerous a requirement for most taxpayers, especially the smaller ones, and perhaps was regarded as a waste of time in view of the practical impossibility of making any headway against the governor's absolute powers. The result was that, in a population of just under one million souls (at least half of whom were 21 and over), the island's voters' lists totalled less than 40,000 electors, with some parishes having only around one thousand each.

Political apathy was further encouraged by the rigid social stratification that had prevailed, almost unchanged, since the Emancipation. Skin colour determined social class rigidly. At the top of the pyramid were the British governor and the white officials plus the native whites who engaged mostly in commerce and large-scale farming. This was the ruling class that governed the society benevolently but firmly. Below them was stretched a long list of variegated shades of colour, hopelessly mixed, their social station fixed by their darkening descent to the black skin. In descending priority after the whites were the near-whites, their pink complexions attracting the colloquial description of muste-fino; then came the mustays, swarthy but still lighter in colour than the brown-skinned mulatto who could split into an endless variety of groupings, depending on the extent to which their *"white"* blood was reflected in the quality of their hair. Then the lower social echelons grew progressively darker in hue, including the sambo with his less than jet black skin matched by rough but curly hair; and finally at the base of the pyramid were the blacks, distinctive as much for their colour as for their poverty. All along the line a bit of money helped to maintain a social station and even to promote a little mobility. Nor did the minority racial and ethnic groupings — Jewish, Chinese, Indian, Lebanese — disturb the social pattern, for these minorities tended to segregate themselves in their enclaves, dedicated privately to money-making and the preservation of their dimly remembered cultural traditions.

Chapter 3

Such a society could hardly be homogenous, though on the surface it appeared tranquil and law-abiding. The gulf between the blacks and the rest of the society was wide and seemingly unbridgeable. Protest movements against living conditions at the base of the pyramid since the turn of the century had been sporadic but insignificant. Between 1907 — the year of the great earthquake that devastated Kingston — and 1908, printers and tobacco workers staged a series of strikes on their own. Nothing came of their efforts.

Labour unrest of a more pervasive and sustained nature took place during 1918-1920 in the wake of the World War 1. Returning soldiers of the West Indies Regiment were barely restrained from a mutiny. In April, June, July and December of 1918, a rash of strikes blossomed forth in Kingston and spread to outports and other areas in the country.

In April, a strike of sugar workers at Vere in Clarendon erupted into a riot which was quelled by police. Three persons were killed and a dozen wounded. Fire-fighters, dockworkers, railway mechanics and the match-factory workers in Kingston and the banana workers in other categories in outports, in turn resorted to strike action.

A. Bain Alves, cigar maker and founder and president of the newly launched Longshoremen's Union No.1 of the Jamaica Federation of Labour, petitioned the Governor, Sir Leslie Probyn, to give official recognition to Trade Unions. Probyn, a Liberal, responded and the Trade Union Law was introduced into the Legislative Council in March 1919, given second and third readings in June, and was proclaimed on 25th October 1919. It conferred legal status on properly registered Trade Unions and protected them from criminal prosecution as conspiracy or unlawful combinations operating in restraint of trade. It did not, however, release them from liability for suits for damages as a result of strikes, nor did it legalize peaceful picketing.

Strikes again occurred during July and December 1919, the most serious and protracted being among railway workers and shopmen who tried to derail the train by removing rails between Highgate and Albany.

A dispute between the tramway company and its employees also led to the establishment in January 1920 of the first conciliation and arbitration board in the island's history.

During the next decade and a half, labour unrest took the form of occasional strikes and riots. In February 1924 cane-cutters at Fellowship Hall demanded higher rates for cutting canes. Police promptly arrested 9 ringleaders who were dubbed "trouble-makers". In June municipal workers rioted at Darling Street and banana workers at Port Antonio went on strike. Railway workers and then later in the year construction workers on the Bog Walk Road struck for higher wages.

Occasional stoppages also occurred during each of the years 1925 through 1929 among longshoremen, sugar-workers, cigar-workers, banana-workers and construction workers. In 1932, there was a serious riot at Grantham Estate and strikes among banana workers in Kingston and outports.

If working class protest appeared to be muted over the period 1924-1934, it may be attributed to preoccupation with Garveyism and the safety release provided by emigration.

This trek from home, which remains to this day the single most dynamic force in our society, has a history that is worth recording for a proper understanding of the relative tranquility during the greater portion of the period between the two world wars. We have to go back to the 1880's to trace the genesis of this population movement. The Board of Visitors of Government Reformatories sent in its annual report to the Government in May 1887. Normally it would have been a routine report; but in this instance it sounded the alarm in respect of increasing juvenile destitution and delinquency. As a result, the acting Governor, Rushworth, set up a commission *"to inquire into the condition of the youth of the Colony, with a view to the devising of means for the protection of the destitute, the training of the ignorant, and the reclaiming of the idle and criminal"*.

One of the witnesses before the commission was William Lee, a prosperous Kingston auctioneer who also carried on a furniture and cabinet-making business. In the course of his historical evidence as to the reasons for the increase in vagrancy, Lee told the Commissioners: "I think the causes are very remote. You have to go back to 1845 to discover them. Up to that time Jamaica had been gradually getting over the shock she received at the time of emancipation. Then came the disastrous Sugar Bill of 1846 (which put slave-produced sugar from Cuba in direct competition with free-labour sugar produced in Jamaica and the rest of the West Indies) which has to a great extent been the cause of the misery that has since prevailed throughout the length and breadth of the island. It was then that sugar estates were thrown out of cultivation and the whole industrious habits of the people destroyed. After that Sugar Bill came into operation, say in 1846 and 1847, there was not a day's work to be found for a carpenter or bricklayer throughout the length and breadth of this city. Many thousands of tradesmen and labourers were forced to seek employment elsewhere; they went to the Isthmus and completed the Panama Railway, and nearly all of them died there, indirectly the victims of the free traders and sugar refiners of England".

How many Jamaicans passed through this safety valve? In 1853 and 1854 the trek was rising steadily. In the latter year the figure reached 3,000 male Jamaicans, attracted by the day labour rate of 2/6 for work on the railway. But when the Railway was completed in 1855, a total of about 12,000 Jamaicans had found self-satisfying employment at liberal pay rates on this historical rail link between Panama's capital city and its Caribbean seaport, Colon. Many of these migrants returned home when the railway was completed: some to resume their old occupations, others to use their savings to invest in land and set themselves up as freeholders. But with the passport restrictions still in their infancy, a fair proportion of them remained in Panama to form the nucleus of a Jamaican colony, mainly in Colon, that was destined to grow as that country's geographical location proved a magnet to European exploiters seeking a short passage to India, China and Japan.

The magnet drew the first iron filing in 1879 as the French diplomat, Ferdinand de Lesseps, the hero of the Suez Canal, led a consortium of European capital bent on cutting a waterway across the Panamian waist from the Atlantic to the Pacific. This huge construction project beckoned to the enterprising, adventurous Jamaicans. The second big migration wave rolled again to the Central American republic that had been created under the inspiration of Simon Bolivar, greatest of the American liberators, half a century earlier under the name of Colombia. It took de Lesseps ten years to run out of money and abandon his creative dream. But in the last year when he ran up the flag of failure, 25,000 Jamaicans were in gainful employment with his French company. As in the 1850's, most of the Jamaican migrants returned home, nourished by their adventure and turning its proceeds to good use by further investment in land, and as before, a portion of their number remained to swell the Jamaican colony in Colon.

At the turn of the new century, the opportunity for two more large migration waves opened up in the same central region and

Jamaicans splashed abroad in greater numbers than ever before. The Americans sought to take up the project where de Lesseps had left off. But the negotiations with the Government of Colombia got into a sticky deadlock. The American patience ran out and their President, Theodore Roosevelt (who was later to earn the nickname *"Bull Moose"*) put together a combination of local politicos, tossed out the recalcitrant ruling group and carved out a new republic that was given the name of Panama. Roosevelt quickly concluded a treaty with the new governors that gave the Americans the right to dig a Big Ditch to provide ships with a short cut from the Atlantic to the Pacific. The treaty gave the Americans control of the waterway in perpetuity with the Panamanians guaranteed modest royalties from the total amount of fees charged for the shipping operations. The construction of this Ditch, requiring hordes of labour, proved a godsend (literally) to our Jamaican people who were straining to escape the frustrations of low wages and primitive living conditions in the urban areas and on the decaying sugar estates. In the twelve years that the construction work lasted, upwards of 50,000 Jamaicans found gainful employment at wage rates that were more than twice the prevailing rates in their homeland.

Meanwhile a parallel migration outlet was opened up in Costa Rica, an adjoining republic. The American engineer, Minor Keith, had completed the ill-starred Costa Rican railway, then, looking for new worlds to conquer, turned to the planting of bananas along the diluvial coastlands of the republic. The trickle of Jamaican workers who had helped him build the railroad swelled to a torrent for his banana growing; and when the Lindo brothers, leaders of a noted Jamaican family, followed the *"green gold"* path blazed by Keith, a further 40,000 Jamaicans found employment on these sprawling banana plantations. In lesser numbers Jamaicans also migrated to Colombia, Nicaragua and Honduras where the banana growing craze had spread, and also to Cuba where the sugar industry was being developed by similar mass production. In all these places, the Jamaican worker earned a high reputation for skill, industry and thrift, virtues that were not fully displayed when he worked in his own country. The British Colonial Secretary in Jamaica, Sir Sidney (later Baron) Olivier, whose Fabian Socialism made him perceptive of social conditions and sensitive to the under-lying conditions, probed the reasons for the difference in attitude of the Jamaican worker at home and abroad. He put the question to Captain L. D. Baker, master of a

Boston trading schooner who had founded the Jamaican banana trade. Olivier gave Baker's illuminating analysis in his book, **Jamaica the Blessed Island,** published in 1936.

"His answer was that the Jamaican in Costa Rica worked hard and earned a good wage, and that he simply would not do the same in Jamaica. Captain Baker was a first-class employer and his judgement and word reliable. The determining circumstance was that in Costa Rica every labourer had to work for the full working week, with the alternative of being dealt with as a vagrant. Men who could not show that they had any means of subsistence or work to do were taken by the police to the lock-up. Employers were asked if they wanted labourers, and how many. The men in the lock-up were then allotted to them; if they refused to work, and were foreigners, they were shipped out of the country. The labourer on the farms habitually worked six days in the week. He had no provision ground to look after, and bought his food. The conditions of settlement in the coast belt of Costa Rica rendered the enforcement of such a vagrancy law possible there, but it would obviously, apart from considerations of policy, have been quite impossible in Jamaica, where the existing pretty strict vagrancy law, framed with a view to repressing praedial larceny, had never been of such practical use.

"When a Jamaican went to work on the Costa Rican plantations he accepted conditions more exacting, and according to his ideas more akin to slavery, than those which he would have consistently refused to accept in Jamaica. He received compensation for this in the wage of a dollar a day, which the difference in the return to labour cost made it impossible for the Jamaican planter to. pay, but which at five and a half or six days a week paid for allowed the labourer a good margin for saving. The meagre savings which he could make out of his Jamaica wages for three and a half or four days a week were not worth troubling about, and he spent all he earned, only working for as much as he wanted for weekly expenses. Moreover, he was not at his home, in the land of the free, and everyone else that was working in Costa Rica was in just the same position. No fox had a tail. He was not under contract, but he was under the practical compulsion I have described".

The labour disciplines that were valid in Costa Rica were duplicated with local variations in other countries of Central America: in Colombia, Nicaragua and Honduras where the banana craze quickly caught on, luring perhaps more than 10,000

Jamaicans to make a good thing out of touching the *"green gold"*. And in Cuba, too. Only in this case the lure was sugar. The Americans had just completed the final expulsion of the Spanish from their last colonial footholds in Cuba and Puerto Rico. But the Cubans had supped satisfyingly of the revolutionary brew fermented by Jose Marti and Antonio Maceo, both of whom had fallen on the field of battle against the Spanish a few years earlier. The Cubans showed that they were not prepared to swap the decaying Spanish autocracy for the rising, vigorous American colonialism when the alternative of freedom and independence was within their grasp. By 1902 they had established their independent republic, with the twin crops of tobacco and sugar as its economic mainstay. Tobacco was the small man's crop, requiring an artist's care for each individual plant, as Marti once described it, *"With his protecting hands, against the excessive heat of the sun, the treacherous cricket, the rough pruner, the rotting damp"*. But sugar was a different matter. It was the ideal crop for virgin lands and masses of labour. Cuba had the virgin lands in abundance; so American capital pushed in to create a new bonanza in which Cuban labour was beefed up by further mass migration from Jamaica. Within a decade Jamaicans had established yet another colony outside their homeland, this time mainly in Cuba's Oriente Province in the south. The numbers were around 30,000 souls.

Between Emancipation and the end of the first world war, a total of perhaps 200,000 Jamaicans, mostly ex-slaves and their dependants, migrated to countries washed by the Caribbean as well as to North America. This was the safety valve that relieved the pressure of social protest within Jamaica, save for the exceptional upheaval of 1865. But the Caribbean economies have traditionally been reactors rather than innovators of their own history. Totally, abjectly dependant on Europe and North America, the Caribbean has always shuddered in the wake of the slightest bowel-motion of these advanced metropolitan centres. So when the great postwar depression swept over North America and rattled into western Europe in 1929, its reverberations shook the Caribbean (as much as Central and South America) to their foundations. In the ensuing conditions of hardship, new waves of unanswerable nationalism surged to the surface. Jamaicans, foreigners in these Spanish-speaking countries, found popular feeling turned against them in their isolated enclaves. As the Johnnies-come-lately, they had to be the first to lose out as far as jobs and social services were concerned. Economic pressure plus direct legislation in many cases forced our Jamaicans to look homeward. The trek back began by 1930 and was continuing in 1934 — the year that Bustamante returned. The returnees brought new, republican ideas of protest with them. They brought a lingering taste of the better life — certainly better than anything Jamaica could offer them. They also brought home their new work disciplines and skills. They melted into the large body of the Jamaican masses. But if their fellows who had stayed home were the dough, they were the leaven to give vigour and shape and purpose to the end product.

Between 1934—1937 Bustamante stalked about the island like a tiger in a cage. His quiet money-lending business in Duke Street was growing steadily, despite the high interest rate of one shilling in the pound, per month on unsecured loans. Meanwhile, he had invited a slim, brown-skinned girl, Gladys Longbridge, to give up her cashier's job at the Arlington House restaurant where he lunched daily and became his private confidential secretary. He was cutting a dashing figure as an elegant man of the world: debonair, sharply-suited, with charming if exaggerated manners and a clipped, foreign accent which combined to make even a moment of dalliance a memorable occasion for the shy, modest girl from Westmoreland. But from the start there was little of dalliance between them. Their regard for each other was mutual. And so the very nature of his business fitted into the personal initimacy of the one-room office they shared for the greater portion of each day.

But overlaying this steadily growing prosperity that money-lending, mainly to underpaid junior civil servants promoted, was a restless irresistible urge to be involved in public affairs. Bustamante gravelled at the grassroots of the society. Every day was a revelation of how Quashie really lived and reacted. At first his own feelings were of amazement, then they turned to indignation and very often they came to boiling point; and finally, perhaps without his realising it, a sense of deep compassion welled up, matured and then flowed out of his personality in an endless wave that was to run through the rest of his years.

Chapter 4

Alexander Bustamante returned home to settle down in 1934. But then his family was scattered. His father and mother, Bobby and Mary Clarke, had deserted Blenheim in Hanover after Old Man Shearer's death. They had come up to the capital city, Kingston. His sisters had chosen separate, individual paths. Maud was married to a dark-skinned methodist clergyman, the Reverend Austin Evelyn, and all her time was taken up with rearing their son and two daughters, little knowing that the boy was destined to become a full Professor of Physics at McGill University in Canada in her own lifetime. Louise had married a Grenadian, Bertie Purcell, and together they had founded the Purcell Home for Boys in Highgate. There they were rearing their son, Donald, preparing him for his career as one of America's outstanding motor engineers. Iris had gone off to New York as a Hospital Nurse; while Herbert had gone to Boston in search of a better living. He remained there continuously except for a short visit home at the time of the Independence celebrations in 1962. He died soon after.

Bustamante's half-sisters, Ida and Daisy, had also trekked to the city. Ida had gone into private employment, while Daisy had married a man named Cotterell who died shortly afterwards, leaving their only child, a sprightly girl, on her hands. Meantime Iris, Bustamante's full sister, had sent out funds from New York for her parents to buy their own home. This they secured on a lane off the Lady Musgrave Road in upper St. Andrew. But Bobby died in 1924 and was buried at the Provident Methodist Church cemetery on the Hope Road not far away. Iris, home for the funeral of their father, stayed on to make arrangements for the future of her widowed mother. Together, they decided to sell the suburban cottage and buy a small farm in the hills of Portland where Mary, forever a simple country girl, could pursue the placid life in the rural environment she loved so much. But the year of Bustmante's return home, Mary got seriously ill. Louise brought her mother from Portland to Highgate to stay at the Purcell Home. But Mary never got really well again and the following year she died and was buried in the church cemetery in Annotto Bay.

But Bustamante was little concerned with family matters. He was seeking to find an outlet for his voracious energy in public affairs. He began harmlessly enough with letters to the Jamaican Press. Conceivably, this chore could provide his first, preliminary public platform. He staked out the public media with calculated caution, concentrating on the **Daily Gleaner**, whose solus position in the daily newspaper field gave it a virtual monopoly in the country. He kicked off with a careful comment that lent comfort to a proposed demonstration by the city's unemployed. He described the demonstration as *"a proper method of calling attention to conditions or grievances"* and, warning that *"force is a dangerous thing"*, he cautioned that *"those who possess force should be careful how they use it"*. Equally he admonished the demonstrators against resort to violence. Then he laid down a principle that carried political overtones: *"It is no good telling people that government is not concerned with them, for government tells them what to do and what not to do, where and what to buy and how much to pay for it. Government poses as a paternal government and as one looks to one's natural parents, so the people look to the government when they are unable to help themselves"*.

This first essay in journalism disclosed a vigorous, original style, backed by an advanced social conscience that made him one of the few among a breed of letter-writers whose main pre-occupation was with religious and sports issues. The public reaction to this letter was so favourable at the level of the society that he was aiming at, that on the day of its publication, Bustamante followed up with a further development of the same theme. It was the year (1935) of the Silver Jubilee of the British King, George V.

He proposed that every employer of labour "employ one extra person, however small the wages might be, when we are able, and give this a try for, say, six months" as the start of a *"Silver Jubilee Employment Campaign"*. Nothing came of the idea, of course, but the seed was falling on fallow ground.

In May 1935, Bustamante turned his attention to proposed legislation seeking to protect native industry by curbing imports but creating local monopolies that drew his fire: "The result of monopoly is always the increased suffering of the unfortunates. Industrial dictatorship suits but two classes who are much in the minority, viz: a few large, privileged capitalists and some smaller traders who have already established themselves in some form of industry and would rather bear the punishment of the devil destroying the entire world if he could, than to have their own countrymen start similar industries".

As the year wore on, Bustamante threw a steadily widening net. He joined in the discussion of the proposed quota of banana shipments between the United Fruit Company and the Jamaica Banana Producers Association, holding a middle course between the competing claims. When a JBPA defender took up the cudgels against this middle course and demanded to know who was this Bustamante, he spilled out for the first time the legend of his early years: "I was born in Hanover. At a very tender age Spain became my home. I served in the Spanish Army as a cavalry officer in Morocco, North Africa. Subsequently I became an Inspector in the Havana Police Force. Recently I worked as dietetic in one of New York's largest hospitals. Bustamante is a lonely fighter; he belongs to no organisation or club. He fights on the side of fairplay. Not only that, he fights on the side of his enemy if he is on the side of justice, without fear of any consequences whatever". He opposed a proposal to import a plumber, decried the Governor's intention to restrict the use of drugs in hospitals on economy grounds, tore into the Custos of Westmoreland for calling illegitimate children "bastards".

After publicly thanking a well-known merchant for helping him when his car ran out of gasoline on the Stony Hill Road, Bustamante rushed to the defence of the Pope for not intervening in Italy's rape of Ethiopia, then rounded on the Governor for imposing a new tourist tax which he saw as *"driving away the tourists from our shore".* He made a strong plea for investment in slum housing, penned a long, glowing tribute to the city's Mayor H. A. L. Simpson. The Governor brought forward new tax measures that worked out at 4½d a week on businessmen, to repay an official 12 million loan. Bustamante shrilled for a full month, denouncing this as a *"disaster"* and the elected members who supported it as *"betrayers".* He took issue with two anonymous columnists on the rib-tickling issues of Bathless Americans and Jim-Crow hotels in England — a hilarious dialogue that carried him to the end of 1935.

Curiously enough, what proved to be the first wave of labour unrest and a *"dress rehearsal"* so to speak, of the working class revolts which took place in the West Indian territories including Jamaica from 1937 to 1938, passed by without Bustamante being involved. In Trinidad in July 1934, hunger marches precipitated strikes in the Oil Fields. In January — February 1935, St. Kitts had its turn as striking sugar workers were insistent and threatening in their demands for higher wages. The Governor summoned a British warship from Bermuda as well as police reinforcements from Antigua. The ensuing clash between police and strikers left three dead and eight wounded.

Jamaica was next and then later in the year there were strikes in British Guiana, a serious disturbance in St. Vincent and a coal strike in St. Lucia.

In Jamaica, at the outport of Oracabessa in the northcoast parish of St. Mary, banana workers became incensed over the introduction of workers from the nearby town of Port Maria. On the 14th May, 1935, they paraded in protest with sticks and other make-shift weapons.

They were quelled by police action and Government officials accused *"outside agitators"* of inciting workers. One week later, violence flared in Falmouth and other northcoast outports. Wharf workers tied up city traffic to forestall strike-breakers being brought in. One died in the collision with local police. It would seem that these two incidents did not make the impact they might have, because they were localized and did not extend to Kingston as was to be the case in 1937 − 1938.

One thing that the labour unrest did point up, was the dire need for workers' organizations to facilitate the management of labour protest and the processing of grievances. A new initiative at trade union organization was taken by A.G.S. (Father) Coombs, among others. Alan George Coombs served first in the Police Force for about 3 years and then in the West India Regiment for about 5 years. When he left the Regiment in 1927, he had attained a rank of Lance Corporal. In 1936, Coombs formed the Jamaica Tradesmen and Workers Union (J.W.T.U.), a blanket-type union into which all categories could be organized without too much concern for occupational identity. The J.W.T.U. derived its support initially from artisans and their helpers concentrated in Kingston, as well as waterfront workers, but soon Coombs, an austere man with a forceful personality, attracted a modest following and the union expanded slowly into St. Catherine, St. Mary and to St. James, attracting dockworkers and agricultural labourers. As his union was not financially viable, Coombs supported himself by working for the Public Works Department as a road contractor. The J.W.T.U. was registered on 29th June 1937 and remained the rallying point for agricultural workers until 1938.

By 1936 Bustamante's fame as a letter-writer was well-founded. He displayed a lively, original wit and a courtly regard for his adversaries. The **Daily Gleaner** and the weekly newspapers continued their liberal attitude of publishing everything he wrote. And his net was still widening. He built one letter around his own rhetorical question: *"Why are foreign Bands allowed to perform in this Island when there are hundreds, if not a thousand native musicians unemployed here?"* He mourned the death of King George V *("Long Live the new King!")*. He defended the morals of Jamaican women, later made a special appeal to dark-skinned women to take a more active interest in sports. He waxed like a medical expert in condemning the proposed siting of the T.B. Sanatorium on Wareika Hill at the eastern end of the city. By the middle of the year his letters were growing shorter, more punchy. He penned an open letter to the Members of the Jamaica Agricultural Society, supporting the appointment of H. H. Coote as Bee Instructor. He joined issue with the Gleaner's Editor who had assured the public that, in case of war, America would protect Jamaica. He encouraged a popular demonstration for the arrival of the British politician Lloyd George. He commented vaguely on the Spanish civil war, made a special plea for *"the forgotten needleworkers"*, joined the crusade against the proposed metering of domestic water supplies in the city. On the last day of the year he was in full cry against metering.

The next year saw the beginning of the second wave of the upheaval which marked the birth of the modern era. During January and February 1937, there were frequent reports of hunger marches, strikes and sabotage by discontented workers throughout the island. The J.W.T.U. led by Coombs expanded its organizational activities and the ranks of membership swelled. It was claimed that in one section, the Spanish Town Section, membership had reached the formidable figure of 2,000.

Bustamante's letters to the Press were fewer as he turned more of his attention to travelling through the countryside, holding small, private meetings. But he found time to add to the legend of being a trained dietician by expounding expertly on the cost of food in Jamaican hotels as compared with that in the Canary Islands. He jumped to the defence of the *Daily Gleaner* whose monopoly position was being threatened by the establishment of a new daily, the **Jamaica Standard**. He had a kind word of praise for Lady Denham, the Governor's wife. Then in March 1937 the upheaval began hesitantly. More than one half of the workers at Gray's Inn sugar factory in Annotto Bay struck for higher wages. When they threatened to become disorderly, the police had to be brought in to protect the workers still on the job. Within the next few months, the upheaval started to churn in the city as the unemployed staged noisy demonstrations. In August, ex-service-men from the first world war clashed with the police as they tried to march on King's House to protest low wages and unemployment. They were dispersed by the police and 23 of the marchers arrested. Banana workers at the outports of Montego Bay and Oracabessa brought loading operations to a halt. And all over this hung the prospect of new municipal and parochial elections.

In Kingston, the waterfront was soon tied up by a strike of Stevedores and before long throughout the Island crowds of labourers armed with machettes and sticks faced heavily armed police squads.

Bustamante appeared on a platform in Kingston making fiery speeches in which he claimed an attack had been made on his life because of his association with the cause of the working man. In the trade union field, Coombs sponsored a number of meetings in the hope of establishing effective unionism but no satisfactory formula to restore peace could be found.

Bustamante associated with Coombs on the platform of these public meetings and, appreciating the opportunity for contact with the masses, Bustamante accepted Coombs' invitation to become Treasurer of the J.W.T.U.

Early in September 1937, Bustamante, Coombs and L. W. Rose (a Garveyite and Secretary of the Spanish Town Division of the J.W.T.U.) were accorded a tumultulous welcome at a public meeting in Montego Bay. From press reports it was clear that Bustamante was a major drawing card. In a letter published in **Plain Talk** September 11, 1937, Coombs paid tribute to Bustamante as *"a man with a human heart"*. He traced the founding of the J.W.T.U. in May 1936 and explained that he had invited Bustamante, whom he knew only by reputation as a letter-writer and speaker on public affairs and was reportedly a rich man, to support the Union and the cause of labour. Bustamante had come forward when other capitalists had not and his name was helping to swell the ranks of union membership.

The J.W.T.U. seemed poised at this time to play a significant role as well in the pending municipal elections in Kingston. Prospective candidates angled behind the scenes for Coombs' support. Bustamante shot off a letter to the **Daily Gleaner** in which he cautioned: *"The leaders of the union should not use any influence whatsoever with their members to vote for any candidate who is either afraid or ashamed or has not enough interest in labour to fight for the union openly"*.

The public reaction to this letter whetted Bustamante's

appetite for a more significant role in the new trade union — his first contact with a labour organization.

Bustamante put a delicate proposition to Coombs: if he would turn over the presidency of the union to him, he (Busta) would finance a vigorous campaign out of his own pocket to establish the union on an island-wide basis. Attracted by the financial implications, Coombs allowed his hesitancy to be overcome. In a letter dated 12th October 1937, addressed to the editor of **Plain Talk** (now regarded as an important labour weekly), Coombs proclaimed that he had voluntarily relinquished the presidency to Alexander Bustamante and would become first Vice-President. Members of the Executive, however, soon began to have second thoughts. Moreover, Bustamante found a formidable contender in the person of Hugh Buchanan, General Secretary of the Union and a long-time Marxist, whose ideological fastidiousness was revolted by the idea of a money-lender leading a workers' union.

Buchanan had attended a meeting of the Communist International held in Hamburg in the early 1930's. A tough-minded mason by trade, he had made a good impression among the comrades in Hamburg as a promising torch-bearer in the English-speaking Caribbean, and even if he did not make much use of it, he was the only Jamaican with a direct link in the money-line that led from Moscow.

Buchanan had teamed up with Coombs to help organize the J.W.T.U. He had also teamed up with a printer, Stennett Kerr Coombs, to publish the openly Marxist **Jamaica Labour Weekly** on luridly coloured newsprint. With the growing disenchantment over Bustamante's presidency of the J.W.T.U. and with Coombs having second thoughts as to whether he had made a good bargain, Buchanan organized a counter-coup which ended in Bustamante having the traumatic experience of being expelled from the Union.

Throughout November and early December, the **Daily Gleaner** and other weeklies carried letters of recrimination between Coombs, Bustamante and other trade union colleagues and well-wishers. Bustamante alleged that he had resigned from the presidency because of irregularities in the union's financial affairs. Union officials replied that he could not have resigned from a post in which he had not been confirmed, and accused him of exacting his *"pound of flesh"* for his financial contributions.

Chapter 5

Meanwhile, social unrest was visibly quickening. *"Little"* strikes were popping up among banana workers on various estates. The strikes were spontaneous and called in lightning fashion.

On 1st December, a new union, the Jamaica Hotel Employees Association, was registered. The city's retail clerks, euphemistically called *"shop assistants"*, were growing restive with their demands for minimum wages and shorter working hours. They rushed into a new clerks' association organised by a trio of middle-class leaders: Florizel Glasspole, a city accountant, Erasmus Campbell, an aggressive barrister who had resigned his job as an agricultural chemist in the government service and gone off to Britain to get his second profession, and Ernest Rae, a burly cricketer who reached Test status and who was also helping to organise citizens' associations to bring a new look to municipal politics. The clerks were planning to close the retail shops during the Christmas shopping season. A lean Christmas was narrowly averted when the Legislature bowed before their militancy and passed a Shop Assistants Law that prescribed restricted trading hours with provisions for a weekly half-day holiday.

During his brief honeymoon with Coombs in the Jamaica Tradesmen and Workers Union, Bustamante had laid out in one of his letters a clear-cut philosophical base for unionism. He wrote: "The objects of unions are: to get the people to unite in masses to contribute their little money for cases of emergency so that in the time of this and the time of that the union will have money to work for the interest of the members the way the Executive Committee thinks best; that there should be labour representatives who will represent the cause of labour not alone to their employers but to Government; to work for better understanding between Labour and Capital; to work for better wages, better working conditions, and to work in the interest of the unemployed to seek ways and means to obtain them work".

"A labour union is nothing more than the working people's club where they can unite for one common good, for one common cause, so that they can bring their grievances to their officers. Union members, if you want to be successful, you must remember that you must follow your officers and must not expect them to follow you, and for that reason the officers should be men of intelligence, honesty and reliability. You, the workers, are seeking justice from your employers, then to accomplish this you must also measure out justice and fair play to them, however, cruel they may be."

"You must never even (go) to strike against them without first bringing to their notice, through the right channel, that you are dissatisfied, and even when capitalists may refuse to do anything, it is your duty to persist in an amicable way to gain your ends before you resort to strikes. Strikes must be the last thing on your minds, they must only come about — if they have to come — after we have exhausted every arbitrary method with capitalists and Government and both turn their backs on us; then and only then it is time for us to make up our minds not alone to starve for one common cause, but if needs be to die for it with a smile upon our quivering lips. I do not agree with these strikes that have been going on here and there; it might help a little section, but it will prevent progress of the union, and I want the workers to know that if they want my help they will have to follow my advice. I do not intend following theirs".

But Bustamante was at odds with the temper of workers when he exhorted them to exhaust orderly procedures of grievance administration before resorting to strike action. The masses once aroused and set in motion, have a mood, not a mind. It was clear that disorganization had already set in. Workers remained confused, inarticulate, and without effective accredited representatives. The year ended ominously with a strike of agricultural labourers on the Serge Island Sugar Estate in St. Thomas in the eastern end of the island.

Chapter 6

1938 was the Red Letter Year. For three patient years earlier, Bustamante had been hammering home the principles of unity — trade unionism — in his long letters in the **Daily Gleaner**. Now, the message had got through. But the masses of people, once aroused and set in motion, have a mood, not a mind. In the first week of this upheaval year, the mood registered hot. At Serge Island sugar estate in St. Thomas, over 1,000 cane cutters, having idled their machettes, marched into the factory compound with a shrill demand for an increase on the 10½d a ton they were being paid at task rates. They demanded 2/- a ton for cane cutting.

The police and estate guards — really a private army — were hastily summoned. The tensions were held within non-violent bounds, but the demonstrations continued for three days around the perimeter of the factory. Then the floodgates burst. The strikers retaliated violently when the police tried to break up their groupings with flailing batons. The day's count of casualities: 34 workers and one policeman injured, 60 strikers arrested.

That evening Bustamante, with the faithful Gladys Longbridge at his side, motored to Serge Island to support the strikers' demand of 2/- a ton. The estate management made a counter-offer of 1/- a ton. After nearly a week's haggling, the cane cutters accepted the counter-offer reluctantly; for at the end of the haggling, a side effect of the strike was concluded in the awesome court of law in Morant Bay when fines and prison sentences were imposed on 21 of the 60 strikers charged with various misdemeanours. So the uneasy peace settled over the estate area, a mere six miles from the stomping ground on which Paul Bogle had launched the Morant Bay Rebellion nearly three-quarters of a century before.

But where Paul Bogle and his mentor, George William Gordon, had been fighting almost in isolation in 1865, the Serge Island incident was merely a symptom of the countrywide restlessness that was climbing to boiling point. The action came next in Westmoreland, about 180 miles roadwise from the eastern to the western section of the island. Tate & Lyle, the British sugar refiners with global activities, was pushing into Jamaica in the mid-thirties to infuse a new faith in the future of the sugar industry as a profitable channel for capitalist investment.

Robert Kirkwood (who was to be knighted 20 years later by the British Queen), a relative of the Lyle branch of the two-member family of sugar refiners, had come to Jamaica to head the subsidiary, West Indies Sugar Company, that was designed to spearhead Tate and Lyle's intrusion. Kirkwood acquired 24 small, near-bankrupt sugar estates scattered through Westmoreland and Hanover and welded them into a giant sugar central factory at Frome, six miles from the Westmoreland parish capital, Savanna-la-mar.

But this promise of large-scale production of this plantation crop held out little prospect of improved working and living conditions. Wage rates were abnormally low. Where the Government's daily labour rate was 3/3 on roads and other public works, the estates' daily labour rates were 1/- to 1/3 for man and 7½d for women. Human relations were often harsh and brutal at the levels of lower management. Wage bills were paid only on Saturdays, often after the village shops were closed, thus making it difficult for the workers to make their food purchases. Child labour was rampant and helped to keep the wage rates depressed. Working hours ranged between 12 and 14 daily for a six-day week, with no overtime rates for Sundays and public holidays. In crop time the estates were served by hordes of migrant labour that came from as far as 40 miles away and therefore had to be housed — in primitive, unfurnished barracks. The mood in Westmoreland registered boiling point.

A former Director of Agriculture, A. C. Barnes, was induced by Kirkwood to become estate manager of the giant Frome central factory. Its large-scale sugar production raised the obvious question of the new company's ability to pay higher wages for all its workers. Without any outside prodding, the manual labourers on the construction project nearing completion sat down on their jobs. To send their message that they were demanding higher wage rates they massed in the estate compound. Barnes got his counter-message to the strikers. Instead of words for a dialogue, he directed estate security guards and the police, rushing in droves, to disperse the crowds of strikers.

But these were a new breed of Jamaican workers. Many of them had recently returned home from Cuba and Panama and Colombia and Costa Rica where they had drunk deeply at the well of republicanism. For those three patient years, Bustamante had been hammering home the principles of solidarity and united action. His message had got through to them in western Jamaica. Once their solidarity was assured, they stood up manfully to the police and the guards without flinching. Fourteen strikers gave their lives in those bloody battles; scores were injured and even larger numbers were arrested.

On the opening day of the strike the news was flashed to Kingston. The next morning, April 9, Bustamante headed out of the city for Frome in his stylish Willys-Overland car. At his side was the ever-faithful Gladys Longbridge. Busta's arrival brought a temporary lull in the fighting in the estate compound. Busta conferred with the leaders of the strike. They spelt out in specifics their demands. Then Busta selected a small delegation from among them and sought an interview with Barnes. At first Barnes refused to see them. But Busta hadn't driven the 150 miles from Kingston only to be brushed aside contemptuously like that. He literally forced his way into Barnes' office, demanding to be heard. He set out the workers' demands in staccato details. But Barnes was unyielding. He refused even to discuss the workers' grievances. Bustamante and his delegates returned to the main body of the strikers and reported the negative results of his representations. So the fury was renewed within the estate compound. Only, this time it ranged further afield: to the outlying sections of the estate, along the dusty roads, into the numerous sub-offices scattered for miles within the estate.

The fury raged for a full week. Special constables were recruited and commissioned, mainly from the ranks of the frightened *"middle"* (white collar) class. By that time Busta and Gladys had returned to the city. For days and nights Busta prowled the North Parade in the downtown city holding meetings on St. William Grant's platform. Both of them stalked, trudged through the city's waterfront, whipping up the dockers to protest against their hourly wage rate of 11d.

The social barometer registered flashpoint. The convulsion came on May the 23rd.

Chapter 7

That morning May 23, 1938, the eve of *"Empire Day"*, Kingston's dock workers gave the lead for the action. They stopped working on the waterfront. For a couple of hours they milled about the wharves – excitedly but resolute. Then some of their number drifted along Port Royal Street, Harbour Street. The word spread through the city's shops and offices. As the word went, other groups of manual workers like the dockers followed their lead. By mid-moring, the economic life of the city braked steadily to a halt.

So panic took over the city. Businessmen hastily pulled down their wholesale and retail shutters. Government offices gaped sullenly with idle hands. Private offices prudently closed their doors and sent their staffs home. Police on the streets were recalled to their central station for closer re-grouping. The British soldiers at Up Park Camp were alerted for likely acton. As the number of striking workers mounted, squads of them pushed out from the main streets to encourage their comrades on the outskirts to walk off their jobs.

Alexander Bustamante, his shirt open down to his navel, his shirt-sleeves, like his mop of shaggy hair blowing in the wind, headed for the wharves, in the city's westend. On the way he met a large group of dockers heading out to King Street. Few words passed between them. After a few minutes, Busta whirled about, heading the column of strikers. The vanguard of the workers had found a leader – and Bustamante had found a Cause.

Near Duke and Harbour Streets, a white-faced police inspector, W. A. Orrett, packed a gun in his fist as a dozen red-seamed constables backed up behind him. They advanced menacingly on Busta and his back-force of strikers. It was the day's first confrontation. Only six feet divided them when the two groups halted. Busta told Orrett: *"If you're going to shoot, shoot me!"* and he pushed forward his bare chest invitingly. But the police moved aside and the tight-lipped strikers resumed their march up Duke Street with Busta leading the way.

With the police withdrawn from point duty, the city's traffic descended into chaos. But a civic-minded band of strikers quickly took over traffic control: directing cars and horse-drawn buggies and the public tram cars past the clogged street intersections. But the small group that is the lunatic fringe in every crowd soon had a field day. They roamed the city's back streets and lanes. They menaced the small shopkeepers, mainly Chinese, looted their shops. More than anything else, they cause the barometer of tension to rise towards anarchy.

As the day wore past dusk into evening, the crowds still milled along the streets. They were consumed with a sense of elation — a sense of achievement — and self-confidence poured into spirits that had been inwardly hesitant that morning. They didn't know what tomorrow would bring. They weren't to know that Busta would soon be arrested for sedition — that he would be caged in a prison cell for a week before being freed by a High Court judge on a second legal manoeuvre — that Norman Manley would intervene with a conciliation offer that was to be refused until Busta was released.

They weren't to know these things that fateful evening in a pre-public holiday in May. But they had made their bid for freedom. After this, things may get better — or perhaps worse. But Jamaica would never be the same again.

Chapter 8

It was now May 24, *"Empire Day"*. Despite the public holiday, the city was in the grip of a paralysing general strike. That afternoon Bustamante and St. William Grant were arrested and held without bail. The charges against them included that of SEDITION. J. A. G. Smith *("Jags")*, the older of the two leading counsel and the black eminence on the elected side of the Legislative Council, filed a writ of Habeas Corpus in the High Court, seeking the release of the two men on bail. Smith was instructed by Ross Livingston, the solo lawyer who was the nephew of Sir Noel Livingston, senior legal partner of Livingston & Alexander located in Duke Street in the city.

Norman Manley, the younger but the better jury-hypnotiser of the two leading counsel, trekked to King's House to see the Governor, Sir Edward Denham. Manley knew how these things could be managed. He tried to persuade Denham to withdraw his directive to the High Court to refuse Smith's application. Manley failed. The directive was issued from King's House. When Smith's application for Habeas Corpus came before the High Court, the British judicial puppet, Mr. Justice Cluer, refused the application for the release on bail of Bustamante and St. William Grant.

But Manley, the brilliant cajoler with sweet, logical phrases, was single-minded in his persistence. A few days later the legal genius returned to King's House. By that time, the striking dock workers had made it clear that they wouldn't return to their jobs, despite the offer of increased wages, until Bustamante was released. This time Manley was more persuasive with Denham. Between them they fixed up a new scenario that was quickly played out.

Smith renewed his application to the High Court for the release of the two labour leaders. A new judge was put in to hear the application: the Jamaican judge, Mr. Justice (Acting) Bertram Burrowes. Denham issued a new directive to Burrowes to grant the application. Manley gave evidence that Bustamante's release was essential to the restoration of social peace. Burrowes granted the application, but stipulated that the two labour leaders should not address any public meetings.

So Bustamante and Grant walked out of the General Penitentiary on Tower Street at the eastern end of the city to inhale the wind of liberty. They were now free men. So, of course, they went straight to the city's waterfront to hold several victory meetings. Later, the charges against them were quietly dropped.

Now, thundering out of the swelling chorus of faith, loyalty and frenzy came the refrain that was to remain imperishably for generations to come: *"We will follow Bustamante till we die!"*

A Personal Postscript

1965 was the centenary of the Morant Bay Rebellion. Bustamante had had a serious stroke (minor) and two eye operations the year before. But on June 14, 1964, he made a manful appearance at the Queen's birthday reception at King's House. He stood firmly in the midst of scores of his friends and admirers, the cynosure of observing eyes, as he traded witty sallies across the broad lawns. But for the rest of the year there were whispered reports that Busta wasn't getting better in his robust-looking health.

In the new year I made a news commentary on RJR on January 22. I told the public:

"I hear from my usually reliable sources that there are some important changes coming in the Cabinet and these seem to indicate the inner resilience of the JLP, on a level with that shown by the PNP in reaching a consensus on its new policies.

"Mr. Donald Sangster, I'm told, is to give up as Minister of Finance and devote his full time to being Deputy Prime Minister. As such, he will take on the day-to-day work of the Prime Minister who will be 81 next month. I also understand that Mr. Roy McNeil will go from Home Affairs to Finance, though I have no information as to who will replace him in Home Affairs.

"These changes, I'm told, will go into effect after the Budget is settled by Parliament in April. Their new effect will be that, for all practical purposes, Mr. Sangster will be our Prime Minister and Minister of External Affairs and also Minister of Defence, though in all important decisions he will pursue his natural best of close consultation with Sir Alexander as he always does.

"Mr. Sangster may not provide Jamaica with inspiring leadership: he's not that kind of personality; but this much can be said for him: he will provide safe, sound leadership and if the Cabinet follows his guidelines, the Government will lose much of its whimsicality and pursue a reasoned, orderly course that our intelligent citizens can anticipate. Under Sangster's leadership, we may not as a people achieve anything significant or meaningful, as some of us think our potential deserves; but we'll continue to believe, illusory or otherwise, that we could amount to something, though we're not sure what that something is or could be.

"If these changes go through, they should be reflected in a

more bracing posture on the part of the Government. This would be an added improvement to its new attitude of reconciliation with the teachers and the organised farmers — a reconciliation that has considerably brightened the political prospects for 1965. But the changes should also halt the current of rumours flowing through PNP circles that we're likely to have a snap general election some time this year.

"These rumours have been building up for a month now. They've alerted the PNP leadership to tighten up its organisation — just in case. This may be a good course for the party; but it can hardly be conducive to national stability if one party is continuously braced to fight an election campaign, especially in our particular circumstances in which trade unionism is so integral a part of politics.

"As I see it, the elevation of Sangster to an even higher reponsibility than he now bears on his youthful, active shoulders would be clear proof that the JLP had decided to dig in for the remaining two years of their parliamentary term; and if I judge Sangster's temperament aright, I think he will be more concerned with going ahead with a number of popular showpieces that are also of advantage to the national interest and thus using the two years to create a public image for himself and the JLP that will stand them in good stead in 1967. For even now, it's becoming clear that Sangster himself will be carrying the burden of JLP leadership in 1967 as far as the general public is concerned. Walk good, my friend."

In a smarting reply to my broadcast, Prime Minister Bustamante wrote me on his official letter-head which I treasure fondly. Here it is now:

PRIME MINISTER'S OFFICE,

P.O. Box 512,
Kingston,
Jamaica, W.I.
January 23rd, 1965.

Dear Sir,

Yesterday, in your commentary over the radio, you were heard to say that from your "usual reliable source" you were informed that after the Budget there will be a Cabinet re-shuffle and that I am handing over my duties to the Deputy Prime Minister, including the Ministry of External Affairs; also that Mr. McNeil will be performing the duties of Minister of Finance.

Your "reliable source" in this instance is the father of mischief. If ever I decide to make changes, no "source" will ever know until the changes have been made, as under the Constitution I am under no obligation to inform anyone except the persons concerned, and through courtesy the Press, and, of course, my Union which plays a most important part in the election of Members to the House of Representatives in my Party.

For your own information, I have no intention of giving anyone any more authority.

You also made reference to my age. Fortunately for the Country, my age does not represent my mental and physical capacity, which, in my opinion, is superior to some of the youths who write and speak mischief.

Will you be good enough to have that commentary, which is without any foundation whatever, retracted?

Yours truly,

Alexander Bustamante
Prime Minister

Frank Hill, Esq.,
21 Merryvale Avenue,
Kingston 8.

Through The Exit Door

The two reports came at the same time officially during the week ending January 27, 1967. They were announced almost in the same breath by the acting Prime Minister, Mr. Sangster, at a public meeting in the Halfway Tree park. And it was difficult to decide which of the two announcements held the edge in public attention.

Mr. Sangster said that the Prime Minister, Sir Alexander, had decided to retire from active public life after the next elections for reasons of ill-health; and then he went on to declare that the new general elections would be held on February 21.

The public was not caught entirely by surprise; for the Gleaner had beaten the gun at the start of the week with published forecasts of the announcements. When Parliament was officially prorogued on Tuesday at midnight, most people knew that the forecasts were straight from the horse's mouth.

The two announcements were twins: one flowed directly from the other. Had the Old Man decided to stay in harness on a part-time basis as he has been doing these past two years, we would have had a later date fixed for the general elections, perhaps June or July. For in that case the date-fixing would have been mainly his responsibility and it is not part of his character to make quick gambles where political power is concerned.

But Busta's decision went the other way. He faced his own position courageously in his farewell message. *"I have come to this decision,"* he wrote, *"because my ill-health, caused through overwork, has not sufficiently improved to continue the rigours of political life and Government."*

Once this decision was made, it followed as a matter of course that all future decisions concerning the JLP and the Government would have to be left to Mr. Sangster and his Cabinet colleagues who would have to take over the political responsibilities fully.

Sangster's key position as Minister of Finance led him in the direction of early elections. The reasoning stemmed from the Government's budget deficiencies: the national difficulty of raising loans for capital development in markets that were growing increasingly short of capital, in relation to the demands made on them by developing countries like ours.

This was no fault of the Government's. It was a global problem facing the capital markets in the western world. Demand has become greater than the supply of money. So money was tight in that interest rates have become high: too high, in fact, for any rational Government to depend on too heavily for its loan funds.

In our case, we are just over £8 million short in our capital budget. This situation is not going to improve in the new financial year that begins on April 1. It is more likely to deteriorate. That means that the Government — a JLP or a PNP Government, it does not matter which — will have to dip back into our local resources for the money for capital development without which we cannot improve the living standards of our people.

But the local capital market is quite small. It could not possibly provide the £20 to £25 million required for the capital Budget in the new financial year. Much of this new money will have to come from additional taxation. But though everyone recognises that taxes have only a one-way street upwards to climb, most everyone has a personal distaste for digging deeper into their pockets to fill the public purse.

Mr. Sangster, every inch a politician, knows this only too well. So he reasoned that it would be political suicide for his party to raise taxes in April and then go to the country for a vote of confidence in June or July. Far better, he decided, to go to the country first, win a confidence vote, he hopes, and then administer the bitter tax pill.

This was legitimate electoral strategy. So the date of February 21 was chosen because it had some sentimental significance: it was close enough to the 83rd birthday of the retiring Prime Minister — February 24 — for the JLP to exploit the nation-wide affection for Busta by asking the voters to give the Old Man a suitable birthday present in the form of a JLP victory at the polls.

Curiously enough, the JLP have shown from the line laid down at the mid-week meeting at Halfway Tree that set their election campaign fully in motion that they intend to fight as much on Busta's personality as on their record over the past five years. But was there an anomaly in the fact that the party was appealing to the voters in the name of a leader who would no longer be there to lead them?

With Busta's retirement offstage, we now have the opportunity to take the full measure of this great man.

Busta was essentially a warrior. He understood only too well that in a society like ours, progress — social progress — comes with struggle and even sacrifice. He didn't work this out from any finely spun theory: he knew it from instinct. So he was all set for a fight for the clean, fair fight. And if the going turned rough, he could be just a little rougher than the best of them.

Busta was the organiser of our social revolution. He didn't create that revolution in 1938. That was done by the people themselves in their instinctive mass protest against poverty and hopelessness. But once the people went on the march, he put himself at the head of the line and, in the split second of communication between leader and followers, the people lodged their abiding faith in him.

Busta was the best type of Jamaican leader. He never ran too far ahead of his people. More than all, he learnt along with them from every living experience and then in turn used his great gifts to draw the lessons for them. So year after year he became the teacher who learnt as he taught; and so there was no end to the growth of the man.

For the first five years of the struggle, Busta concentrated exclusively on moulding and shaping the social revolution through the trade union he founded to bear his name. His organising tactics were pragmatic, ready to hand. Sometimes it was the sudden, massive strike, then the sitdown around the conference table to bargain from strength. At other times, it was the protracted process of agitation among groups of listless workers as he dangled a long list of demands in their faces and whipped up their spirits for the fight.

For five years Busta held suspiciously aloof from the political struggle for nationhood. He didn't grasp the political concepts at first, clothed as they were in philosophical abstractions. But when the first wind of political change began to blow in 1944 with the PNP's achievement of a new constitution based on universal adult suffrage, Busta knew instinctively that the Freedom Train was about to make a significant turn. His response was simple, direct, to the point. He gave his union a political manifesto, added a branch structure that he called the Jamaica Labour Party, and climbed easily into political office.

With this step, Busta completed his dominance of Jamaica's public life: a dominance that he is only now surrendering. He carried the country through the first constitutional change that provided for a ministerial system of responsibility. Then after 10 years in office, he fell slightly from popular favour and was succeeded by his cousin, Norman Manley, the most brilliant of our intellectuals.

But even through the seven years that he spent in Opposition,

Busta maintained his dominating influence. His cousin, Manley, was the orator who hitched fine phrases together in undulating tones. But Busta was the mesmeriser who wove hypnotic spells by taking simple truths and repeating them over and over in altering cadences.

When Manley polished the constitution in two strokes as many years apart to bring home rule to Jamaica, Busta grasped the full meaning of nationhood. In that flash of insight, he worked out for the first time a political philosophy that could be translated into action. For him, to be a nationalist was to repudiate any ties that limited the sovereignty of his nation. So Busta set out to detach Jamaica from the federal union that he had helped to create, though in lukewarm fashion, a few years earlier. The popular vote backed his lead; and so we came to Independence.

Busta was an authentic, Jamaican original. He was too creative to be hindered by orthodox forms and traditional precedents. No one but Busta would have dared to combine the office of Prime Minister with the presidency of one of the two rival trade unions. No one could have done so without getting his lines fouled up and without breaking faith with either of his two offices.

The key lay in his great humanism: the great heart that reached out to people with unerring instinct, rather than the agile head that rationalised and hesitated in confusing doubt. But he took people as they were, understanding their needs, their hopes as much as their prejudices. By remaining within the framework of his times, he was able to impact these times with an indelible stamp that bore the major traces of his own personality.

I have known Busta intimately ever since he set up his loan office in 1934. I have fought on a picket line beside him. I have battled with him on the other side of the political fence. I have wrangled with him, laughed with him, lectured him, loved him. For he made the history that I have lived through these past 30 years.

He often told me — and as often repeated in public — that he would live to be a thousand years. Most people put this down to vanity or to his fear of death. But Busta lacked that kind of empty vanity and needless fear. I know — and he knew too — that he can never die; for he has carved himself for all time into the history of a new nation and its people. He is one of our immortals.

(from a Radio Commentary by the Author)

Modern Jamaica In Miniature

The social upheaval of 1938 brought two fundamental changes to Jamaican society. The first was the radical re-ordering of the economic structure. This was shown in the establishment of the wage-earners' right to organise and join trade unions. This basic right levelled out the economic inequities that had steadily grown up between employers and wage-earners since the Emancipation a century earlier threw the labouring men on the free market with nothing to sell but his labour power.

The second fundamental change was slower, but no less radical. It was the building of a new political society in which the British colonial authority was replaced by the democratic suffrage of the whole adult electorate who freely chose a Government responsible for their welfare.

The first change made its impact immediately in 1938, with the organization of the Bustamante Industrial Trade Union. The second change was a slower evolution to national Independence in 1962. Alexander Bustamante was unquestionably the organiser of the first. He was also the kingpin in the chain of events that brought the second to its final flowering.

Up to 1938 Jamaica had never lacked ideas and causes, many of them alien and quite irrelevant to the development of the nation's human resources. What Jamaica lacked up to then were the fixity of purpose and the continuity of organised action to put those ideas to practical work and to give those causes a purposive Jamaican character. These deep-rooted defects stemmed in large part from the carefully nurtured sense of inferiority that had been instilled in the ordinary Jamaican all through the 300 years of British colonial rule. An offshoot of this popular inferiority complex was a natural distrust of leaders who were suspected of not having a total commitment to the people's welfare.

Bustamante steadily countered the national inferiority complex with his daily organising strategy of workers' demands, face to face collective bargaining including militant strike action, then amicable settlement. And he beat down the offshoot of suspicion and distrust by proving his total commitment by his personal courage: by his being sent to a detention camp at the height of the war in Europe; by his bold challenges of authority on the streets, on the picket lines, in the many marches and demonstrations he led and the many more speeches he made to bolster the people's spirits.

Bustamante cultivated a sense of equality and self-respect in the Jamaican People. He helped to brace Jamaican shoulders to fight on their feet as men rather than to grovel on their bellies like serfs. By his militant admonitions and actions, he helped to erode the former class distinctions that were based primarily on the colour of a man's skin. And together with all these imperishable improvements in the human spirit, Bustamante helped to provide through his organised trade union activity a limitless horizon of practical economic gains for our wage-earners that make the pre-1938 period seem like an age of barbarism. The ascending levels of wages today, the expanding list of fringe benefits that include vacations and sick leave, workmen's compensation, medical schemes, pensions and severance payments — all these were hardly a deeply felt aspiration before 1938 overwhelmed Jamaica.

The fact that the Trade Union Movement has made organised labour into the dominant force in our society today is a living monument to Bustamante's sustained, self-sacrificing public service over 30 arduous years. And that work took on a universal significance in two important aspects. One, it brought the people of the largest English-speaking territory in the Caribbean into the mainstream of modern democratic development; and two, it resulted in the first successful organisation of rural farm workers into modern trade unions in the British colonial empire.

Alexander Bustamante was essentially a pragmatist in political matters. In the first flush of years that succeeded 1938, he concentrated single-mindedly on the job of ensuring a firm, lasting foundation for the trade union movement, allowing himself only minimal attention to political developments. But when the British conceded the Jamaican claim to self-government with a new Constitution based on universal adult suffrage, that would eventually lead to Jamaican home rule, Bustamante extended the frontiers of his activity by organising the Jamaica Labour Party to bring the wage-earning class more directly into political action. And in the first general elections under that new, democratic Constitution in 1944 he asked for and received, on behalf of his party, a clear, popular mandate to guide the Jamaican people as a whole along the road to political maturity at the same time that he was leading the wage-earning class to a widening economic equality.

That popular mandate was renewed five years later. During this second term of office under Bustamante's leadership, Jamaica took two major steps forward. One was in the economic field — the purposeful steps towards industrial development that has added new skills to her people and accelerated pace to the growth of the national economy. The other step was in the political sphere — the introduction of the Ministerial System that put real power and responsibility into the hands of the elected representatives of the people to develop and administer policies that are devised to preserve and expand the people's welfare.

But during this period, too, Jamaica was prodded by the British Government to join with the rest of the English-speaking Caribbean into a federal union. Bustamante and his party expressed strong reservations about such a federal union. But the movement towards federation gained momentum when Bustamante's party lost the elections of 1955 and the P.N.P., originally founded in 1938 to win home rule for Jamaica, sought to have Jamaica gain her independence through an Independent West Indies Federation. The Federation was formally inaugurated in 1958 with the explicit pledge that Independence would be achieved five years later.

But federal strains and tensions soon developed between Jamaica and her new partners. The Federation was barely two years old when Bustamante struck at the Gordian knot that was tying Jamaica into a bundle of frustrations. He ended the bi-partisan attitude towards the Federation by announcing that, if and when his party were entrusted in the future with the reins of Government of the country, he would take Jamaica out of the union. The governing P.N.P.'s reply was its decision to put the whole federal issue to the electorate in a Referendum: should Jamaica continue in the Federation or secede?

The Referendum was held in September 1961. Bustamante and his party counselled a negative vote at the polls and that Jamaica should afterwards proceed to Independence on her own. The result was a substantial vote in favour of secession from the Federation. The arrangements were quickly made for the fourth and final amendment of the Constitution to bring Jamaica into full independence. Now general elections were fixed for April, 1962, with Independence Day four months later. It seemed natural that, since Bustamante's counsel was given popular approval in the Referendum, he and his party should be mandated to lead the country through its first years of Independence. And so it turned out in the pre-Independence elections, and Bustamante became the first Prime Minister of the new nation.

A long, crippling illness struck down Bustamante in the middle of his new term of responsible office. On the eve of the second elections in independent Jamaica early in 1967, he was forced into retirement from public service. But time cannot dim the priceless value of that service, spanning nearly 30 years, that shaped the cause of the working people and nurtured the progress of all the Jamaican people to freedom and independence.

Our history will unquestionably confirm him in the twin roles of Organiser of the Social Revolution and Father of the Nation. These add up to merit him the title - National Hero.

*Reproduced from a painting by
Schliefer in the Author's Collectio*

A Personal Memoir

by Norman W. Manley

The Government Public Relations Office published an official brochure on Jamaica in Independence Week. It is a record in brief of the new nation and it contains short accounts of the lives of the six Jamaicans whom it would be natural to think of in connection with our Independence.

The Prime Minister, Sir Alexander Bustamante, is of course among the six and this piece of his life begins with the following passage;

"The Hon. Sir William Alexander Bustamante, Prime Minister of Jamaica, was born at Blenheim, Hanover, on February 24, 1884. He attended Government Elementary Schools and then, at the age of 15, he was adopted by a Spanish Mariner and taken to Spain, where he lived for many years.

"His education was continued through private study in Spain, culminating in the Diploma of the Royal Academy of Spain for commercial Spanish, Italian and Portuguese."

This is carrying a joke too far and "Public Opinion" has thought it a public duty to set the record straight by a short factual account of the early life of Sir Alexander. This is probably a case where truth is stranger than fiction and the facts better than any version of the myths which have been so carefully (or is it cautiously?) built up.

At the end of this article we append a family tree diagram which shows how Sir Alexander Bustamante comes to be half-cousin to another Jamaican also numbered among the six, the Leader of the Opposition – N. W. Manley. The Prime Minister had a sister, Miss Ida Clarke who was Matron of the Verley home for aged, poor gentlewomen until she retired in 1962 well over 80 years of age. She died a few months ago. Then there is Mrs. Vera Moody and Dr. M. M. Manley, sisters of the Leader of the Opposition, who can speak with authority of the period immediately before Alexander Clark, as he then was, left Jamaica; and of course there is the Leader of the Opposition himself who knows all the principal events in the Prime Minster's life from he first left Jamaica in or about 1905 until his final return in 1935.

Here are the facts in bare outline.

Sir Alexander was born at Blenheim in 1884 (at any rate that is the date he gives, we have not checked it).

His grandfather, one Mr. Clark, had one son only and when the grandfather died his grandmother married a second time to one Mr. Shearer who was an Irishman and became owner of Blenheim, was father of several daughters including Margaret Ann Shearer who became a Postmistress at Porus where she married Mr. Thomas Albert Samuel Manley, a produce dealer of that town.

Mr. Clark, son of the lady who on her second marriage became a Shearer, was himself to marry twice.

By his first wife, he had two children, Ida and Daisy, and by his second wife he had four children who lived to become adults. Louise, Iris and Maud were the girls, Alexander (the Prime Minister) was the boy.

Alexander grew up in Hanover and as time went on his sister, Maud, was adopted into the Shearer family that had moved to Belmont in St. Catherine.

In time Mrs. Margaret Manley, daughter of Mrs. Shearer and half-sister of Sir Alexander's father, took over the management of Belmont property in St. Catherine when old Mr. Shearer became blind and from about 1903 until her death in 1911 she was in charge at Belmont which became a sort of second home for the Clark family. In addition to Maud who was adopted into the household, Iris lived at Belmont for many years and Louise was herself a constant visitor and resident.

It was to Belmont that Sir Alexander, "Aleck" as he was then called, came as a young man in or about the year 1904 and lived for one year training for the job of Overseer.

At Belmont he met and grew friendly with a remarkable young man called David Mullings who began life there as Coachman but was driven by ambition and mental energy to leave for Cuba about the same time as Sir Alexander himself when they both went to seek their fortunes in a land which in those days was a sort of promised haven of hope for so many Jamaicans.

Sir Alexander did well enough in Cuba where he was at one time in the Police Force and where later on he became a Traffic Inspector in a Tramway Company operating both in Cuba and Panama.

Sir Alexander first returned to Jamaica briefly in 1912 when he got married at Marie Villa in Church Street, the home of a family of spinsters – the Plummers – leaving to return to Cuba shortly after the wedding. That was the first of his three marriages.

Between 1912 and 1922 the history runs to earth. There is no one except himself who can say just where he was or what he did in these years between the ages of 28 and 38. Mullings had gone to America where he became a qualified engineer and the first glimpse Jamaica had of Sir Alexander after 1912 was in 1922 when he paid a flying visit to the Island remaining here for just a few weeks. It is the fact that he arrived here from Cuba and returned to Cuba but that is about all that the sources of our information can tell about him at that time.

They do speak however, of his air of prosperity in 1922, of his meticulous care with his dress and of his general stylishness which showed how well he had absorbed the attitudes of a Cuban man of affairs.

Then he dissappeared from the Jamaican ken till 1928 when he was back again, this time making a determined effort to establish a life for himself in this community.

Those were the days when he went into the Daily business and made a seemingly all-out and single handed effort to make a go of the effort. But not for long. Soon he was off again to Cuba and somewhere in the early 1930's he returned, this time with the idea of going into bee-keeping. Many people recall that visit and how short it was and how quickly he left.

It was after that brief episode that he found himself in America, probably via Cuba and it was in America in the early 1930's that he changed his name to Bustamante. In the States he was known, not as Alexander Bustamante, but as Alejandro Bustamanti and there it was that he lived as a gentleman of Spanish origin and birth.

There is speculation as to where the name Bustamante derived and one writer suggests that at the least he must have known some ship's captain who befriended him and whose name he chose. We do not know. What we do know is that the name Bustamante is well-known in Latin American history as one of the minor leaders in the struggle for Independence of the Spanish Colonies.

In America Sir Alexander had a varied career. At one time he was in Boston and there he gave shelter to young Donald Purcell, son of his sister Louise who lived with the Manleys when he was a boy at school and went to the famous M.I.T. Institute of Technology at Boston where he graduated to become eventually a highly placed motor-engineer in the research field.

It was in New York that his second marriage in around 1933 occurred. She was a Canadian Nurse and the record of the marriage is in the Bureau of Health under the name of Alejandro Bustamanti who is described as of Spanish origin.

Not long after he came back to Jamaica to set up business as a money lender under the name of Bustamante. Then began a series of letters to the press which attracted much attention and it will be recalled how long everyone assumed that this was a foreigner come to live among us.

Then came the tensions of 1937 and Bustamante first appeared at Victoria Park under the auspices of the Trade Union that Coombs was then in charge of. Indeed, he was Treasurer of the Union.

Soon he was to strike out on his own in 1937 and 1938. At the age of 54 and after a life that had not involved any intervention in public affairs or in organizations of any sort, he discovered a new range of powers and attitudes and skills and the rest is part of the modern history of Jamaica.

Surely this truth is far more remarkable than the romantic fiction which obscures a true story of how a man late in life and with no props at any time in all his career returned after a life abroad to become a leader in his own land and here to reach the highest that any leader could attain.

Author's Note
(Copy made August 7, 1964)

FAMILY TREE

Alexander Bustamante
née William Alexander (Aleck) Clarke

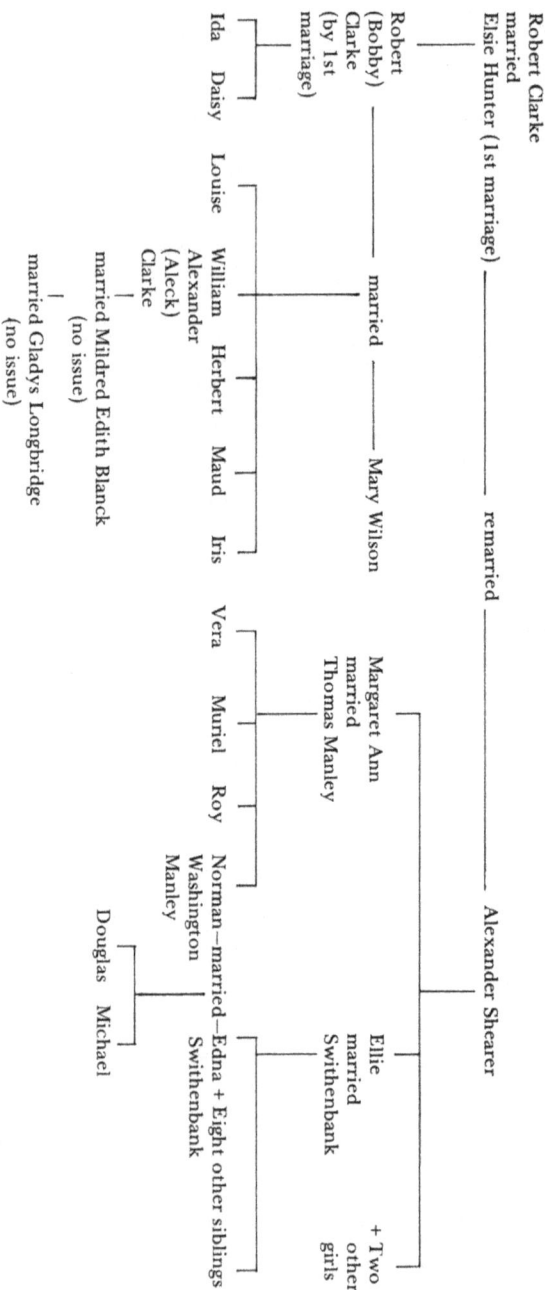

Robert Clarke
married
Elsie Hunter (1st marriage) ——————————————— remarried ——————————— Alexander Shearer

Robert
(Bobby)
Clarke ———————— married ———————— Mary Wilson
(by 1st
marriage)

Ida   Daisy   Louise   William   Herbert   Maud   Iris   Vera   Muriel   Roy

Margaret Ann
married
Thomas Manley

Ellie
married
Swithenbank

+ Two
other
girls

Alexander
(Aleck)
Clarke

married Mildred Edith Blanck
(no issue)

married Gladys Longbridge
(no issue)

Norman—married—Edna + Eight other siblings
Washington   Swithenbank
Manley

Douglas   Michael

NOTES:

1. Alexander Bustamante and Norman Manley were cousins by virtue of their common maternal grandmother.

2. Alexander Bustamante and Edna Manley are cousins by virtue of their common maternal grandmother.

3. Norman W. Manley — Chief Minister (1955–9) and Premier (1959–62) — Leader of Opposition (1949–55 and 1962–9).

4. Michael Manley, Leader of Opposition (1969–72) — Prime Minister (1972). Douglas Manley, Minister of Government (1972).

Bustamante...
His Letters

THE EAGLE: Jamaica's first Chief Minister, Alexander Bustamante, attending the State Funeral of his Minister of Finance, Sir Harold Allan, in Port Antonio in March 1953. On the Chief's left is his nephew-in-law Donald Sangster, the new Minister of Finance; on the right is Frank Pringle, A.D.C. to the Governor of Jamaica, Sir Hugh Foot, immediately behind Bustamante.

THE UNEMPLOYED

THE EDITOR,

Sir,

In your issue of the ninth inst. it is stated that a certain gentleman said that the unemployed should not stage a demonstration and take part in a hunger march but should remain at home and send their leaders to the Corporation.

The latter method of calling attention to conditions or grievances is a proper one as a crowd cannot speak for itself but must do so through leaders to form themselves into a body, and provided this is done in an orderly manner, call attention to, and give practical expression to their condition and needs.

When it was intended to give a welcome to our Royal visitors not only was this done through the people's representatives and the representative of Government by their presence in the form of addresses, but thousands of people lined the streets of Kingston and the roads in the country to add to and confirm the welcome given in their name by the above named representatives.

What is wrong is that in spite of the question of unemployment being made the chief plank on platforms and rash promises as to itself being made to the people when their sufferage was being sought when no relief is apparent or forthcoming the people on approaching those who made the promises are told that the relief of unemployment is no business of theirs but that measures are being taken by someone else to meet the situation.

It cannot be denied that demonstrators conducted themselves in an orderly manner and that the deputation that waited on the Corporation Council expressed themselves very nicely.

It is no good telling people that Government is not concerned with them, for Government tells them what to do and what not to do, where and what to buy and how much to pay for it. Government poses as a paternal Government and as one looks to one's natural parents so the people look to the Government when they are unable to help themselves.

What is also wrong is that when people seek the right of self expression that force should be employed, not to assist them as is done in other countries, to carry out an orderly demonstration and to protect them but to intimidate.

Force is a dangerous thing, it does not always protect, but when used to intimidate sometimes irritates and becomes the author of disorder. Those who possess force should be careful how they use it.

Hungry men and women and children have a right to call attention to their condition and to ask of people fulfilment of promises made to them as long as they do so without using violence or behaving disorderly.

Jamaicans are patient, trustful and law abiding and if properly advised and treated no one has anything to fear. The conditions existing today have not sprung up overnight, but they have been left to grow worse till the situation is now acute. No steps have been taken for their amelioration.

What Jamaica needs is practical and sympathetic men interested in the country and its people and not charlatans and self seekers making long speeches about nothing; men who by their handling of the country's affairs will make such things as hunger marches unnecessary.

'Beware of the Greeks when they bring gifts' and when these gifts turn out to be toads endeavour to climb up a tree.

Happily we have a few men like the Hon. A. L. Simpson in whose hands the interests of the people can be trusted,and who will realise that hungry and needy people will find a way of expressing themselves with the hope that something will be done for their assistance.

I am etc.,
Alexander Bustamante,
1a Duke Street,
Kingston.

UNEMPLOYMENT RELIEF

THE EDITOR,

Sir,

In a recent letter to your valued paper and which you were kind enough to publish I commented on the right of the unemployed to call attention to, by hunger march or any other peaceful means, the fact of their condition with a view to the fact being taken seriously by those in authority and by means devised for their relief.

As I am interested in the matter of unemployment, knowing that its existence is a serious setback to the prosperity of any country I beg to give some further observations in this connection and to point out that any contribution to its increase, even if done unconsciously by employers of labour, is likely to return like a boomerang on its authors.

Through selfishness on the part of some and greed on the part of others and 'follow fashion' in others, there has been a tendency lately to cut down expenses by discharging persons in their employment, not realising that every man discharged robs the community of not only one potential buyer but sometimes a whole family and lessens the spending power not only to others, but to those employers themselves, as the thing goes round in a circle and must inevitably come back to the place where it started, and no one, however smart, can escape the effects of a general condition reacted.

In connection with the celebration of the Silver Jubilee of H. M. the King, H.R.H. the Prince of Wales has started a fund for the youth of England, which scheme is bound to include the question of the relief of unemployment.

In Jamaica, committees have been formed and schemes submitted including one to check the spread of, and relieve those suffering from that dreaded scourge of T.B. This is an excellent and praiseworthy object, and should meet with full public support, although to my mind, this should be a matter that should be taken care of by Government.

Private citizens should wake from sleep and realize that unless something is done for the relief of unemployment and that if the present conditions are allowed to continue for any time the following amongst other necessary actions will be forced on Government, which has to be supported by the people, viz: dole relief, pauper relief, extension of Poor Houses, hospitals, prisons, reformatories and lunatic asylums. These institutions exist mainly as a result of poverty and its attendant consequences of crime and disease. Take also into account the incalculable loss in the degeneration, physically and morally to the generations to come.

It is now worth while to try to devise something to prevent these evils happening and to improve the country. I am suggesting that it is worth while for anyone in position to regard the matter seriously and to make some sacrifice.

I am asking what I consider to be a practical suggestion. I do not wish to have to come to the conclusion that the action on the part of those who are now dispensing with people's services (often those who have served long and faithfully in the past) are prompted not by urgent necessity, but with the desire to grab all and heap up huge profits, and I am appealing first of all to those who are so doing to desist as they are creating conditions that will eventually fall back on themselves.

It is said that a proper element of business thought is to obtain the maximum of service for the minimum of cost, but there is a limit to all things.

I am further suggesting that in keeping with the spirit of and the necessity for sacrifice which is so often preached and so seldom practised, and especially at this time when so much is being said of those who made the supreme sacrifice in the last Great War, and now when the sacrifice of Him who died upon the Cross for us and for the redemption of the whole world is being celebrated, let us stop awhile and see what little sacrifice we can make to make our country better and its people happy.

I am suggesting that a movement be started for each and every one in a position to do so to see if we could not try even if present distressing conditions, but would give us satisfaction in knowing that we are endeavouring to fulfill the prayer often said without meaning to 'Our Father.........Give us this day our daily bread'.

Let us start a 'Silver Jubilee Employment Campaign' and let this idea be put forward in the press and preached from the pulpits and taken up by all charitable and philanthropic institutions and let us see what will be the result. Let us each make a pledge to employ one extra person, however small the wages might be, when we are able, and give this a try, for, say, six months. Most persons could find in their business or elsewhere something one would like to have done but have never given some attention because it was not urgent. I am of the opinion that effort and money spent in this manner would not be wasted.

I am etc.,
Alexander Bustamante,
1a Duke Street,
Kingston,
April 25, 1935.

NATIVE INDUSTRIES

THE EDITOR,

Sir,

Permit me a space in your useful paper to express my opinion regarding the industrial dictatorship which our Governor intends directing towards us.

The writer of this letter has lived in many countries that are ruled under some form of dictatorship and from his experience each kind has had the most disastrous effect upon the middle class of the population and the masses - the very poor ones.

The Industrial Native Protection Bill which the Government is about to impose upon us, is nothing short of dictatorship except that it is robed in a very beautiful colour.

I am not saying that there is any intention to deceive. The suffering of the masses of the people is intense. They are reaching the state of desperation, hungry women and children and men are crying out in their hungry peaceful ways for help from their father - the Government. Is the Governor going to answer their prayer by restriction of industries and trades and thus lessen their opportunity of obtaining work?

The streets of Kingston, the parks and other places are beseiged with beggars; most of them indulge in begging through dire need and poverty.

We who make it our duty to help these unfortunates in the streets and in their homes and realise the need of the people, appreciate the need of unrestricted industries and trade amongst the natives more than anyone that is at the helm of our ship.

One only has to recall the coconut oil industry to see the damage it has done by monopoly. Before this monopoly those who were fortunate to own a few coconut trees could make a little oil, get a few pennies for it and make use themselves of what is commonly known as the 'custard'. Their pigs and poultry are also fed from the by-products.

Can they do things today without risking their freedom?

The result of monopoly is always the increased suffering of the unfortunates. Industrial dictatorship suits but two classes who are much in the minority, viz: a few large privileged capitalists and some smaller traders who have already established themselves in some form of industry and would rather bear the punishment of the devil destroying the entire world if he could, than to have their own countrymen start similar industries.

Let us not consider the two classes above mentioned, but the mass of the people. Let the Elected Members go hand and heart together using every possible peaceful means of protesting against the passing of any Bill which partakes of the nature of 'Hitlerism'.

Let every native whether rich or poor who possesses the sense of justice raise his voice of protest in a peaceful and constitutional manner to submerge this so-called protective Bill which in effect could starve any section of the community.

I firmly believe that the Bill is not intended for that. Nevertheless, however, the power of restriction is used, no man, however astute he may be, is capable of preventing deteriorating results upon unfortunate people.

Were I one of the Honourable Nominated Members, I would not make my will the desire of the sponsor of the Bill. Rather than submit to something against my conscience just to please, I would resign.

What we need in the island is not more men but men with courage, with the spirit of fighting for justice for all and moreso for the less fortunate; independent men who will sacrifice their own interests for their unfortunate sisters and brothers; well thinking men who will speak straight from their shoulders according to the dictates of their conscience and not submit and say 'yes' when their conscience says 'no'.

I am etc.,
Alexander Bustamante,
1a Duke Street,
Kingston.
May 16, 1935.

MATCH FACTORY

THE EDITOR,

Sir,

I notice in your column several letters in support of the so-called Industries and Trade Safe-guarding Bill appearing over the signature, Cecil I. Escala, L.B., Crescent Road, Bournemouth Gardens, Kingston, in the last of which he has the temerity to characterize Mr. Turvill's letter as 'so many sentences of extravagant nonsense'.

Truly there are some who 'rush in where angels fear to tread'.

Might I ask Mr. Escala to enlighten the public as to certain facts?

1. Has he any other address besides the one given in his letters?

2. Has he at anytime been connected with the Match Factory?

3. Has he any interest in the passing of the Bill beside that of an ordinary citizen?

4. Where is he at present employed?

5. What are the "monopolies" that have existed in this country for the past 40 years that The Secretary of State for the Colonies has found it necessary to institute this Bill against?.

I am etc.,
Alexander Bustamante,
1a Duke Street,
Kingston.
May 28, 1935.

BANANA QUOTA

THE EDITOR,

Sir,

There is quite a lot of discussion over the proposed quota of banana shipment. There is a strong defence in favour of the Jamaica Banana Producers Association that unless such a system is established, the company will have to surrender. Now let us analyse the situation from an impartial point of view. The writer has no axe to grind. Let us return to the time when there was no banana company here.

It is a matter of history that the late Capt. L. D. Baker saw the possibility of banana taking the place of the dying sugar industry and started the shipment of bananas to the U.S.A. on his own account by schooners. Later the Boston Fruit Co., was founded and as the venture succeeded eventually their interest was absorbed by the United Fruit Co., which was formed and grew to be one of the largest companies in the U.S.A. A subsidiary company - Elders and Fyffe Limited was founded for the shipment of bananas to the U.K. and the Continent.

Notwithstanding all that has been said about the activities of this magnificent octopus, it cannot be again said that this company aside from definitely placing Jamaica on the map, has done more than any other company to develop the island's resources and to improve the condition of labouring people by instituting medical services, better houses and living conditions and at the time when this was sorely needed. There might not have been the large class of peasant proprietors that exist today had it not been for the activities of this company.

The Jamaica Banana Producers Association was formed as a co-operative movement among the farmers themselves, and as a native concern and to create competition so as to prevent the business falling entirely in the hands of the foreign concern and it is therefore right that it should consider to preserve its existence especially that the Jamaica Banana Producers Association is guaranteed by taxpayers money.

Care should, however, be taken that in such actions the claim of the United Fruit Company should be considered and that one monopoly should not be destroyed for the setting up of another and we should not place ourselves in the position as being regarded as ungrateful people.

What is required is that the affairs of this Association should be enquired into, and things re-adjusted, so that what is stated as the original intention of the Association should be preserved themselves especially the smaller ones.

The time has come when the top-heavy organization with a few people absorbing such a huge proportion of the profit should be altered to a more equal base of distribution.

Everything possible should be done to conserve the interest of the Association without creating undue friction and also without hurting the United Fruit Company.

Listen folks, never forget an old horse that served you faithfully.

I am etc.,
Alexander Bustamante,
1a Duke Street,
Kingston.
June 27, 1935.

BANANA INDUSTRY

THE EDITOR,

Sir,

In your issue of the Gleaner of even date, Mr. Robertson in some parts of his letter has given a vivid illustration of the great economic depression that exists today. In short, he tells us that thousands of banks, business houses - large and small - have closed their doors, in other words gone broke.

The producers of Brazil by Government order have been burning millions of bags of coffee which they have not been able to sell. Ten million bags have been destroyed last year.

I want to correct Mr. Robertson in the latter and not through a feeling of chastisement, that it was not last year that ten million bags of coffee were burnt in Brazil, but nearly three years ago.

Mr. Robertson goes on to say "Think of it. Ten bags of coffee for each man, woman and child of the millions of souls in Jamaica being burnt instead of sold for money."

Now may I ask Mr. Robertson: What is he trying to lead up to with this comparison? For we know as a fact that if we were to cut down all the trees of coffee in this country and bag them we would not expect ten million bags; and if the people of our country would drink more coffee, which I am not advising from a dietetic point of view, we would be able to drink all our coffee ourselves instead of exporting same. This should make it very clear to the public that they should not have the slightest fear that our coffee will ever burn. If Mr. Robertson means to use the illustration of what is happening to the coffee in Brazil to cause an earthquake of fear through the minds of banana growers that the same would happen to bananas in this country, that would be worse than a Judas's kiss, for the entire world does not produce sufficient bananas for such a condition as that which exists in Brazil in respect of coffee. For there is not enough banana lands of fertility to produce such a deplorable condition.

If Mr. Robertson feels that we too might have to burn bananas here, or that as many good bunches of bananas would be rejected after the spider had destroyed the Jamaica Banana Producers Association then it seems to me that this Association would be able to get sufficient good fruit out of the rejected ones. If he is sincere in his belief why does he want a banana quota? Some people write things so that the public should believe in something that they themselves do not believe.

It is unfair and unjust to the other fruit companies, it is unjust to the Government, it is unjust to everyone in this country, except to the few who are drawing this overhead of profit from the J.B.P.A. Associates for anyone to propagate any such vile things as that the other fruit companies intend to destroy the J.B.P.A. Associates so that bananas might return to the 9d and 1/- per bunch, and that they would reject every six or seven bunches out of eight.

Could anyone believe that any such insinuation could come from a righteous person or is uttered for the good of the country? I say no. It is deplorable, monstrous and vile propaganda to the detriment of the masses. And yet it is said, "Do unto others as you would like it done unto yourself". These last words are those of Mr. Robertson. Does he mean that he is doing unto the few men in the J.B.P.A. who have made their company top-heavy owing to the enormous profit at the expense of the banana farmers, moreso to the smaller ones, what he would like done unto his by the banana farmers if he were in the place of those few big men?

There is room here for the other fruit companies and the J.B.P.A. Associates quota. WE DO NOT NEED ANY BANANA QUOTA for the island, what we need is more fair play, more justice, more open market within the island, more competition between ourselves, and less weak-kneed managers and proprietors, so that there may be less need of asking the Governor for protection, thus drawing him into more hot water.

With all this asking for protection, although the Governor surrendered at times to such requests I wonder if he has not been thinking in his heart that we are similar to a bunch of under-fed weak-kneed schoolboys.

Mr. Robertson continues by demonstrating his knowledge of affairs in foreign countries, in Canada, Australia, U.S.A. and Argentine, by saying that millions of bushels of wheat in these countries are awaiting buyers. This is true, but where is the connection between that and our banana in Jamaica when the banana farmers cannot supply the shippers with the amount of bananas they need? If he were writing to the Moors of Rio del Oro in the southern part of Morocco, I could understand that for being ignorant savages cannot compare one thing with another. He goes on to say that hundreds of tons of rubber grown in Ceylon, Sumatra, Java, India and other countries are unmarketed. Millions of gallons of delicious milk of countless farmers have brought no return. What has all this to do with the banana question? Let us hope that he has not tasted this delicious milk for he might become like the "psychologist" who Mr. Turvill claims is a vulnerable glutton for swallowing up two hundred cases of Nestles milk.

He continues: "Farmers in Australia have sheep dying by the thousands". What has that got to do with the question of bananas? Shippers as I have said cannot obtain sufficient bananas here owing to the insufficient production plus destruction through banana disease.

My friends, can you see the right connection of all these things in the different countries? With bananas here? Mr. Robertson asks the question: "What has happened to us?" I will answer that. We have got weak-kneed regarding competition and would like to get the Governor brought down with us.

In one paragraph Mr. Robertson states that the J.B.P.A. is crossing the stream. To that I say whenever rational managers notice their company crossing a stream and is likely to get drowned, they generally throw off their impediments to lessen their burden so as to give them more opportunity to swim. Will the Board of Management of the organization show their interest in their company and the producers by lessening their profits, thereby stemming the tide of discontent that is carrying the Association away?

Mr. Robertson, your abuse of those who have had the temerity to criticize the management of the J.B.P.A. Associates likening these people to Judas, fools, spiders, etc., shows that you have reached your last weapon, and you must by this know that the only effect abuse can have is to alienate the sympathy of those who are viewing the question in an impersonal light.

There are some among the Association's critics who do not own a banana root and are not directly financially interested, but who view the matter in a fair and impartial manner, which they are able to do, owing to absence of financial interests and only interested in the welfare of the country and poor producers.

If I may be so bold as to advise you, let me suggest that you realise that while it is possible to "fool some of the people some of the time, it is impossible to fool all of the people all of the time", that people are becoming thoughtful instead of telling them irrelevant things about other countries, apply yourself in setting your own house in order, reclaiming lost confidence for the preservation of the Association, the good of the banana industry and the benefit of the producers especially the smaller ones.

This can only be done by facing the fact squarely; some people should be willing to remove the weight from on top and to allow the Association to continue on a firm and solid basis. If this were done you would find that the value and usefullness of the organization would be fully realised and appreciated; that it would obtain the full support of the public and there would be no necessity for talk campaigning, quota or anything else to keep it in existence.

I am etc.,
Alexander Bustamante,
1a Duke Street,
Kingston.
July 1, 1935.

WHO IS BUSTAMANTE ?

THE EDITOR,

Sir,

One Mr. S. W. Sharp wants to know who is Bustamante. I was born in Hanover. At a very tender age Spain became my home. I served in the Spanish Army as a Cavalry officer in Morocco, North Africa. Subsequently I became an Inspector in the Havana Police Force. Recently I worked as a dietician in one of New York's largest hospitals.

Bustamante is a lonely fighter; he belongs to no organization or club. He fights on the side of fair play. Not only that, he fights on the side of his enemy if he is on the side of justice, without fear of any consequence whatever. It is characteristic of him to always put his address with his name when writing to the press. I have not seen Mr. Sharp's address in his letter of today's date - makes me think!

Bustamante enjoys the privileges of possessing an irreproachable character, excellent health and a fair amount of wealth. He pays taxes and license and does not work for anybody. He has a little banana but they are on the open market and are going to stay there - at least until the J.B.P.A. Associates are well organized, and until the people have sufficient sense to make such a contract that the pockets of a few will not absorb all the profits so that we should not be like their beasts of burden as is the case today.

With regard to my authority for making the statement I did in a previous letter, I did not get it by sitting in my office at No. 1 Duke Street, but spending my own money travelling by motor car from Port Morant to Negril Point investigating the conditions of the land in which I was born.

In Mr. Sharp's last paragraph he writes: "finally if he has no good authority for making the statement he did he might remain silent". This is what I have done all my life, remain silent in things I know nothing about. But how can I remain silent when this top-heavy organization is being tilted over at the expense of the banana farmers? Why, Mr. Sharp, you could not keep your mouth closed even if you padlocked it.

In Spain I wrote of love and nature's beauty. In Jamaica I can only write of the miseries of injustices and of those persons who are endeavouring to deceive their countrymen and women and of those who are using their evil minds, their wicked hearts to instil in the public that other fruit companies intend to destroy the J.B.P.A. Association. This is untrue.

The great Lord might have John the Devil closed up in some pen, but he certainly has let loose a lot of devils in Jamaica, sowing the evil seeds of injustice for their own personal benefit and their friends, while the masses suffer more and more, too weak to fight for themselves, praying to the Almighty God to liberate them from these of the Devil, some of whose writing make me feel they could better occupy their time by becoming theatrical clowns.

I could write forever on the stupidity of the last paragraph of Mr. Sharp's letter, but the best way for peace is silence.

I am a taxpayer but so many stupid people of this Island believe that unless a man is a taxpayer he has no right to open his mouth, but to become a member of the army of the masses and be voiceless so that evil propagandists like some of those who belong to the Fruit Company whose voices can be heard like a wild cat penned up by a herd of tigers. Is Mr. Sharp one of these? I must now inform the public that everyone who is a citizen whether by birth or naturalization, has the perfect right to open his mouth and let his voice be heard just as strong as if he were a taxpayer.

Good luck, Mr. Sharp. We need more gallant questioners like you, at least I do, for you seem to be comically disposed.

I am etc.,
Alexander Bustamante,
1a Duke Street,
Kingston.
July 3, 1935.

JOB FOR A PLUMBER

THE EDITOR,

Sir,

I notice in your issue of the 8th inst. where you do not accept the recommendation of the Chief Engineer of the Water and Sewerage Board for importing a plumber as a very palatable drink, and it is a reflection against Jamaica.

Honestly, I had to re-read that editorial for nearly everybody in Jamaica inclusive of your paper, merely sit and take such things of vital importance to this country with as much noise as can be got out of a green pea-pod on a breeze-less day.

The recommendation for importing a man for a plumber's job is not alone a reflection against Jamaica but a darn bit of impertinence.

Some people in Jamaica judging certain importations by their performances since their arrival in the Island, are of the opinion that even a plumber's job is too big for some of them.

I would suggest that when the authorities are making up the list for deportation they would see me with regard to the inclusion of certain names.

I am etc.,
Alexander Bustamante,
1a Duke Street,
Kingston.
July 20, 1935.

COST OF MEDICINE

THE EDITOR,

Sir,

In your issue of the 17th inst. a letter appears in which it is stated that the Governor has raised the question of exorbitant cost of drugs, etc., used in the Medical Service of the Island. A suggestion to curtail drugs for the use of unfortunate people who have to seek the aid of Government institutions through absolute necessity, is monstrous.

It has come to this: those in affluence, which include the Governor of Jamaica, can get everything that money can buy, but these unfortunate sick of the Colony are not even supposed to be prescribed for according to the knowledge and conscience of the hospital doctors. Why? Because if the hospital doctors were to accept the Governor's suggestion seriously, after diagnosing they could not prescribe accordingly but would have to think of the cheapest drugs or the nearest substitute. Then if they were to do this just to please the Governor they would be violating medical principle.

What does the Governor know as to the quality of medicine the unfortunate patients seeking medical aid in Jamaican hospitals require, what does he know about the different kinds of medicine or the relative value or the relation of medicine to food? If he knows as much about the relation of food and medicine and the cause of the greater part of the illness in this country, he could not even imagine that too much money is spent on medicine for the poor of Jamaica and I understand that the majority of the people are not even getting the medicines free as in the case of America and other civilized countries.

There would be 50% less medicine used if there were less poverty, better housing conditions and better sanitation, not alone in Kingston, but throughout the entire island. Swamps alone are the cause of thousands of bottles of medicines used annually, if not hundreds of thousands. And what about anemia, tuberculosis, stomach and other troubles the chief of which is poverty and ragged tenement houses with filthy surface drains instead of underground drains.

If these things were to be regulated the hospital doctors would not be so worked to death through the unreasonably large proportion of sickness and disease in this country thus the large sum of money that is being spent and in many cases not to cure but merely to relieve for a time, would not be spent and unless the Governor finds a way to relieve the already mentioned conditions instead of spending less on medicine more Government institutions, more cemeteries, more physical and mental pain among the inhabitants, and more mad houses. In the latter they do not need much medicine they only need more saltfish, and so if all the people could be got in the lunatic asylum, the Governor's desire of economy on medicine would be fully realised.

Before a suggestion is given for financial economy to a place like the Hospital, the person making such a suggestion should first think of the cause of the alleged high cost of drugs used. Did the Governor think of that?

The writer is in no way connected with any hospital in the Island, but he has seen hundreds of people in the outpatients' ward of the Kingston Public Hospital, so many that the sight makes him feel time and again that it is not worthwhile for them to wait day after day to get this little supposed donation of medicine. This is through no fault of the hospital staff, for judging from my experience in a New York hospital where I worked as a dietician and was privileged to go throughout the hospital including the dispensary and outdoor wards where there were thousands of patients daily, it would seem to me that the length of time the unfortunate ones must wait here is due not to the hospital staff but to the hospital being understaffed. It is a crime which the Governor could employ his time to have rectified thus doing some good for suffering humanity. The curtailing of medicine for the poor WOULD TEND TO INCREASE their suffering, and that would not be kindness; that would not be right governing but a gross advantage; and if the doctors were to omit necessary drugs from their lists and substitute them for cheap drugs just to avoid criticism of their department by the Governor, they would not be doctors, they would be weak-minded indeed.

After eleven years experience among young doctors I should have knowledge of the workings of their minds, and I want to say there is not one doctor who would be so stupid as to allow a layman to dictate to him in his professional capacity.

A chef knows just how much cream to be mixed in the milk to make a palatable cream soup, and a novice who knows nothing about it could not rightly presume to tell the chef that he is using too much valuable material. However, it is the way of the world - everybody believes that he knows about the other man's business.

It is hoped that all lists of drugs that have been sent by the S.M.O. at the request of the Governor were sent in Latin.

Whether the Governor realises it or not he has not done himself any good by his criticism of the cost of the drugs to the Island Medical Service, and the psychological effect of it upon the unfortunate sufferers of this country today who cannot afford to seek private medical aid, does not help to strengthen their faith in hospital treatment.

Does the Governor think or does he realise that most of the people pay something for treatment and that those who do not pay, we the taxpayers are paying for, and that no just person would begrudge them the little medicine they get? For, after all, they are not even always cured by it for without corresponding food to each particular case, medicine can only relieve plus a good psychological effect. What will be the next suggestion from the Governor? This last one has left me in a whirlwind of fear.

In conclusion, Mr. Editor, I think the following lines ought to serve as an inspiration:

> "What greater good can man attain
> Than conquest over human pain".

This can only be obtained by allowing the doctors a sufficiency of proper materials, drugs, etc., irrespective of their respective costs.

I am etc.,
Alexander Bustamante,
1a Duke Street,
Kingston,
July 30, 1935.

"BASTARD" CHILDREN

THE EDITOR,

Sir,

A letter appeared in your issue of the 3rd inst. signed by Mr. Hugh Clarke of Westmoreland, in which he said he was the Custos of that parish.

Mr. Clarke stated therein that the Government takes over everyone of the children of the people (bastards etc.,) and educated them free from the age of four. That he was from missionary parents born 66 years ago. That from childhood it was drilled into him that he came into this world to work for the people of this island.

Mr. Clarke also stated that it is to be regretted that the Resident Magistrate for Westmoreland did not enforce payment against a bunch of defaulting tax-payers.

I say it is a blessing that Mr. Clarke was not the judge, otherwise those unfortunate people might have been carried from the side bar of the Court to the Police Station and then to the prison. Then I wonder how Mr. Clarke would take those tears of the dear ones who were left behind depending for food upon those going to prison?

Now, my friends, if a missionary desires you to go to prison for tax, what would be the desire of the Devil? Mr. Clarke's criticism of the judge who tempered justice with mercy by either giving the unfortunates time to pay by not giving judgement against them owing to the lamentable circumstances surrounding some, makes one think of a rebel army in absolute revolt without any true cause.

When such a criticism against a judge comes from a distinguished gentleman as Mr. Clarke, one wonders what is wrong with even missionaries. Save me from them O Lord!

I take much exception to the word "bastard", when penned by a gentleman as Mr. Clarke must be, as there was no rhyme or reason for it to be used as Mr. Clarke had already said that the Government took care of all children. Then why did he have to use the word? Why did he have to remind thousands upon thousands of respectable mothers that they had sinned? If, indeed, they had sinned. Why did he have to remind thousands of respectable men and women that out of wedlock they came? Doesn't Mr. Clarke know that the word "bastard" used in that fashion is a slur, not that I feel that way about it but Society says it is so and you know how it is that sometimes the kettle thinks it is blacker that the pot. Was Mr. Clarke thinking in reasonable fashion when he regretted the Resident Magistrate's action? And may I ask what was really in his mind when he used the word "bastard"?

The reason why I haven't castigated Mr. Clarke thoroughly with my pen is because he stated that he was 66 years old. I respect the 66 and therefore I will not allow my pen to run away with my mind.

When Mr. Clarke says that the Government gives every child a free education, it makes me wonder if there wasn't a ninth night kept beside his dwelling the night before which had upset his equilibrium, for there is no such system of free education in this country. Mr. Clarke stated that the feeble and poor go to the Poor House. It is a Poor House in truth. It is very noticeable from the gate - not one thing cheerful about it, everything seems so cold and when I see the beds and mattresses that most of the inmates just lay upon I wonder why there is not a law to gas them and gas me if lot caused me to go to the Poor House of this Island.

In conclusion, if Mr. Clarke had not said in his letter that he was the Custos of Westmoreland, I would have come to but one conclusion, namely, that it was the letter of an ignorant crank. It is the greatest nonsense I have seen in the respectable and distinguished gentleman and a Custos - a letter which is a reflection against the word missionary, a letter which cannot bring Mr. Clarke any love from the bastards, a letter which cannot bring him any respect from those who come to this world outside of wedlock; for one in nearly every family has erred. That sin, if it is a sin, has been committed through poverty and no person with a righteous heart ever tries to remind others of it.

Let it be fully understood by Mr. Clarke that the writer does not know the Resident Magistrate for Westmoreland, and neither did he come into this world out of wedlock; and the only reason why I have written upon this subject of bastardy is because it is lack of something why he mentioned it that way and that owing to Mr. Clarke's position many who would like to chastise him with their pens are afraid to do so.

What the world wants is no "fraidy-cats", but people who will speak and act according to their conviction. What we want here in this land of mine - Jamaica, is people who will dare to do and will not be frightened at persons because they occupy certain social, financial or executive positions.

"It's a wise child who knows his father." Mr. Clarke should remember in referring to bastards who was it that taught the people illegitimacy - that was not so long ago that marriage was forbidden to them by law.

In the matter of educating the poor man's bastards, Mr. Clarke should deem it a privilege and a blessing to make reparation for the wrongs of his forefathers, and that's that.

I am etc.,
Alexander Bustamante,
1a Duke Street,
Kingston.
August 8, 1935.

KIND STRANGER

THE EDITOR,

The courtesy and hospitality of motorists along the roads of Jamaica is most admirable. When I say motorists I mean from the wealthy towards the poor.

Last night my car stopped in Stony Hill road, she ran out of gas. The first person who passed in his car was Mr. G. M. DaCosta, unknown to me up to that time. He voluntarily stopped and enquired of our trouble. Without the slightest hesitation he offered to return to Constant Spring and bring us gas which he did.

Could anyone expect a kinder act from a stranger? Could anyone fail to appreciate that there was something extremely nice in the inner person of this gentleman? As far as my knowledge goes, this is the kindest act that has ever been done to me by anyone - friend or stranger. In the manner in which Mr. DeCosta volunteered is sufficient proof for me to believe that it is his nature to love to do things for others who are in trouble.

If Jamaica would adopt this spirit it would be a country to love - a country of which we could conscientiously boast of loyalty among ourselves.

I am etc.,
Alexander Bustamante,
1a Duke Street,
Kingston,
August 19, 1935.

THE POPE AND ETHIOPIA

THE EDITOR,

Sir,

One Mr. Thompson and others believe that they could prevent Mussolini going to war with Ethiopia, Rome being the seat of Papacy.

Every man has a right to his opinion, but opinion which is not backed up by reasonable thinking must be considered as foolish. They should know that the Papacy does not any longer rule Government. Once upon a time the Catholic Church ruled supreme over many Governments. Mussolini or any other Latin Ruler would have thought it a mortal sin to act contrary to the Pope's wishes. Spain, Italy and Mexico today are not ruling under the influence of the Church as was the case once. Mussolini being "sin" himself would not tolerate the Pope's intervention.

I am positively certain that if the Pope could prevent Mussolini on his hellbound determination to exterminate Ethiopians, he would, just as he would prevent Hitler from destroying a peaceful race as the Jews are.

It is to be firmly understood that this letter is not written because I am a Catholic, for though I visit all recognised churches, I belong to none.

All churches belong to one God, and whatever their different teachings might be, they are working for the same end - Heaven; and I believe in the same God in whom they believe. But in fairness to the Pope, I will say that the criticism against him is unfair, unjust and unwarranted, for every Christian, I am sure, has a desire to prevent Mussolini, and the Pope is a Christian.

Most recognised religions are serving good purposes and it is not a nice thing to get fantastic ideas in our heads and write ill things about the Pope or anyone else.

The accusation against the Pope is a serious and sad one and I do not care for mixing a wisecrack in the matter; but to show how impossible it is for any one man to prevent Mussolini from his impending assassination of the Ethiopians, I will say that any one man - holy or unholy - who can prevent Mussolini will be able to ride a grasshopper, and, Mr. Editor, you know how difficult the latter would be.

I am etc.,
Alexander Bustamante,
1a Duke Street,
Kingston,
September 20, 1935.

TOURIST TAX

THE EDITOR,

Sir,

Well at last His Excellency the Govenor and his legislature have accomplished something (sigh) by driving away the Tourists from our shore with their Tourist Tax Law.

It is said that we reap what we sow. If this is true, where will we get the strength from to also reap the ills of wild seeds that our Government has sown?

The Bible also says that the sins of our fathers will fall upon us. Now, Mr. Editor, when are we going to get the courage to also hear the sins of our Government?

All these extra burdens need greater faith; and so all we can do as helpless Jamaicans is to pray for wisdom to be instilled in our Government so that we will be able to see danger beyond the stride of their footsteps.

When Governor Denham and his Legislators were enthusiactically contemplating this abnoxious Tourist Tax I wrote a letter to your paper:-

"The present Government of Jamaica climbs the hill from the top; that it was very anxious to have tourists come to our sunny Island, and as an inducement they contemplated taxing their feet."

Such an imprudent contemplation should have been very obvious that it could have done nothing but harm to the Island. The proof of the short-sightedness of this present Government is standing before us like a huge elephant. Some of the Shipping Companies have proved the unwisdom of the act of this Government by cancelling the calls of some ships that would have brought to these shores thousands of tourists who spend thousands of dollars.

When the Governor said to the representative of one of the Ship's Companies that if some of their ships were to be withdrawn from this port there would be others to replace them, he was definitely wrong. The Governor did not think of the Northernmen's spirit, who do not alone resent the imposition but will organize against it to protest. He must only have thought - if he did think - of the non-unity of West Indians, which is one of their failures.

The Shipping Companies have done just what I thought they would do and just what I would do were I one of the Directors.

The world must be nearing its end for the Bible is being fulfilled very often by this Government. It is doing those things which it should not have done, and left undone those things which it should have done.

I hope that the action of the Steamship Companies will serve a good purpose in that the Government will take their action as a bold omen against the Banana Quota.

Here is a suggestion: Unshackle the feet of these happy visitors so that they can walk freely and spend freely. Cancel the tax on their feet. Tax the dogs of Lower St. Andrew and tax every person who leaves this Island on business or vacation, but by all means the Government should undo their error.

Failing to be courageous enough to see their weaknesses, everyone of us should start the ball rolling in the form of a Petition to the Secretary of State for the Colonies to have this law expunged.

One of the ills of Jamaica is that we are always too willing to enter the strife when it is over. Another ill is that we refuse to believe that a hard boiled egg is really hard.

Let us be like most other countries, see the facts and face them. The Tourist Tax is a comedy - The Banana Quota would be a serious drama. Let us fight against them until we can say we have triumphed; we have conquered two great evils.

Mr. Editor, you said in your "Random Jottings" a few days ago, that "there are far sighted people in Jamaica who are telling the people what to do and how to become prosperous". Whatever way you mean it, it's O.K. with me, for your writing is very interesting to me; but I do say and I say so with every sincerity I possess, and though I may say so myself, I possess a whole lot; this Government has erred, more than that it has blundered and I say boldly without any fear whatever, that however bad this Government might be I expected better guidance of our destiny from Governor Denham.

You have praised him from the day he landed here, and that's the only thing I have against you Mr. Editor, for one would think that you would wait until work merits praise.

There can be no greater ill than a shortsighted Government for then all and everyone must suffer.

I am etc.,
Alexander Bustamante,
1a Duke Street,
Kingston,
September 30, 1935.

SAMPLE AND SHOW

THE EDITOR,

Sir,

Jamaica, my land, is a place of sample and show. As you know, a loan of two million pounds is expected. The Council of the Corporation suggested £20,000, Slaughter House, a £30,000 Fire Brigade Station, market, school, the clearing up and rebuilding of the slum areas, roads, bridges, etc.,

If my memory serves me right, not one of these gentlemen have shown business sense of suggesting that money should be invested in Agriculture - Agricultural Loan Board - and nearly everyone of them in referring to the loan always use the words "use" or "spend" which makes me feel that most of them are lacking in that business sense to know that the money is not just for spending like wild oats into the deep blue sea; but to be invested in a way that the Government should get some financial returns, thus lessening the burdens of the taxpayers.

Money invested in the slum areas in the building of houses will be sound investment and all the Governor needs to do now is to have the matter decided upon as to the class of building to be erected and costs, and to start building immediately if and when the money is obtained. When this has been accomplished that will be the right time for the Governor to name a Committee to see that the investment apart from a health point of view and happiness to the poor brings financial returns; for the Governor has already been through the slums and if his visits meant anything materially, he must have grasped the situation.

A suitable market is to be commended for there would be a financial return to the Government if illicit markets outside are not permitted to operate with the new market at the same time.

Roads and bridges should be built for the comfort of all, farmers will be better able to transport their products which would ensure better handling and thus command better prices.

Before a wild goose chase is taken in the dredging of a harbour, they should get down to cold mathematics to calculate if it would be an investment or just money spending which could be invested otherwise with profit. The unfortunate part with most Governments when spending money is that they often think of spending, and never stop to think of it in the form of investment.

A Slaughter House is badly needed in Kingston; good slaughtering means better meat and better health, but it is not far from madness to have suggested the spending of this huge amount for a slaughter house for such a small community. This spending, in truth, is worthwhile for there would be better financial return from what they are receiving today from that source. I have had the opportunity of being in MODERN SLAUGHTER HOUSES and have had the knowledge of the cost of some and if they cannot build a slaughter house for this community for somewhat around £9,700 then we should do without one. Were these men investing their own money, I venture to say that not one of them would sign a cheque for £15,000 or £20,000 to build a slaughter house for they would not run the risk of losing their money. Money borrowed is feather-weight, but when to repay is lead-weight.

A Fire Brigade Station now; an expensive one, gigantic, magnificent in appearance, grander in itself, a great show, a show to hungry people and over-worked farmers who are deprived of the necessities of life is but an extravagant and stupid suggestion. I will be told that there is insufficient accommodation at present to house the Brigade. My answer to that is to buy one of the nearby houses under the Government Land Acquiring Law. I will now be reminded that the Fire Station must be up Orange Street so as to give St. Andrew better fire protection throughout the entire Corporate Area. My answer is: erect a small Fire Station at Half Way Tree and if you want to get at another strategic point, erect another small one at Vineyard Pen. Generals are men who think soundly before they suggest or act and it is our poorness of such quality why our ship, Jamaica, is capsizing.

We have a great show here to be remedied - the show of raggedness and hunger. It is obvious in prominent thoroughfares and it is just as obvious behind the doors of thousands of families who are too timid and too afraid with shame to let the public know of their suffering. The sight behind some doors of mothers with many children is pathetic.

You might ask: how does the writer know? Well, he has penetrated the doors of several of these unfortunates who are his fellow-citizens and has quietly divided his shillings into pennies with them so that they can bite on something beside water while they eat.

I say to all those who have made the wild suggestions to which I have already referred, this is no time to spend money freely which we all have to pay for by extra taxes and these will surely come if you insist on forcing all this reckless spending upon the Governor - he who has already been climbing too many hills and (he) will no doubt succumb to your pressure to the detriment of the Island.

A message to the Government: invest plenty of money in agriculture. Establish an Agricultural Loan Bank so as to induce people to return to the soil, as you cannot send them to the land with 10/- and an acre of land as someone recently suggested in the **Gleaner** unless you want them to live on a quart of corn until theirs is harvested. Put a man outside of the Government in charge, pay him a good salary for his knowledge. Our ship, Jamaica, is capsizing. The mast is one-sided and unless we use wisdom she is likely to submerge like a submarine with a badly defective machinery. Then indeed she will need a wrecker. You should do your utmost to prevent this.

I am etc.,
Alexander Bustamante,
1a Duke Street,
Kingston.

APPRECIATION OF Hon. H.A.L. SIMPSON

THE EDITOR,

Sir,

It is with pleasure that I state that this Island of ours, Jamaica, is most fortunate in having Mr. H.A.L. Simpson as head of the Kingston and St. Andrew Corporation. His interest in doing the right things for the greater good of the greater number of people is very obvious.

One can't help but observe the sincerity which he has instilled in his work as head of the Corporation, and the interest he has shown in those who have put him there.

Whatever his faults might be, I feel that his good outweighs them, and, after all, there is not one perfect being on earth, and I would not like to see him become perfect for that would mean that we would be losing his services here, for he would be on his way to heaven, and although a soul would be gained there, he would be a great loss to Jamaica as a statesman, and a man whose heart belongs to those who are in need.

I certainly admire his forceful personality, his outspoken characteristic, the fearless way in which he speaks out and tackles delicate and serious problems in our country's interests.

Leaders are not only men who win, but men who come to a definite decision and act, even if they might lose. When I think of H.A.L. Simpson, I always remember Roosevelt, for both persons' characteristics, in my opinion, are very similar.

President Roosevelt is a man who speaks out straight from the shoulder. He has a kindly heart and he acts, and H.A.L. Simpson is just such a man.

Good luck with health and long life to Mr. Simpson, not alone for his personal happiness, but also for the happiness of those for whom he undertook the role of City father.

I am etc.,
Alexander Bustamante,
1a Duke Street,
Kingston.

THE GOVERNMENT'S POLICY
The Question of Increased Taxation

THE EDITOR,

Sir,

You wrote - "Laugh or Weep". Quite appropriate, but I would rather say "Groan or Kick"; but whether we laugh, weep, groan or kick, we might not do much, unless there was a Constitution where we could ask for the immediate resignation of the Government. Then, if we succeeded, we could laugh.

I have one God, one soul, one life, and no matter what happens, as long as that life lasts, and as long as the failure of this Government continues, I shall continue to write pointing out its weakness - not because I love to do so, but because it is a duty to my people and my country.

The Bible says there are two places for the sould of man - Hell or Heaven. With a merciful God, I can look forward to Heaven. Can all those of the present Government say so? They who are finishing the last drop of blood of the poor of this Island with extra taxes and child-like suggestions of how the money is to be spent - not invested - should only have the privilege of expecting the wrath of God.

Quoting the Attorney General's remark, he said that those business people who cannot pay 4½d. or 4¼d. per week should get out of business. This was in reference to the hole-in-the-corner businessman and woman, who sells little ice, a few eggs and "Badoo Heads".

I say no Government Official should be allowed to make such a statement. I go further, that they too should get out of the business of the Government. Has the Attorney General any suggestions as to where these people must go after getting out of business? Has he failed to understand that nearly every one of these little businessmen and women have to contribute to the support of some of their unemployed relatives, or does he understand anything at all regarding the deprivation that these unfortunates of this Island are undergoing? Does he realise that some of these same hole in-the-corner business people must live on one 6d. to 1/- along with their family for a long period of three or four days?

I do not write fiction; I write facts, as I can prove what I am saying. Then if a sixpence to a shilling must serve a family for a period of three to four days, from where must they get this 4½d per week to pay taxes? And when they get out of business the only places for them to go are the Mad House, which carries more mad people than any country I know in comparison to its size; to the Poor House which is a disgrace to civilization, or on the Pauper Roll. That was a very undignified and unfortunate remark from such a distinguished gentleman.

The poor will shudder greater under the strain of this undue and cruel taxation, but the rich too will feel it, for there is a depression in business which affects all. Besides, it is reasonable for me to presume that they too are carrying the burdens of supporting unemployed relatives and helping friends and giving to charities.

I am not trying to defend the rich for they are capable of doing so, but at the same time I have not got anything against them, and many of us who are in more fortunate positions than the unhappy ones, and laugh at the idea of people not being able to pay 4½d. a week taxes, have people here or there, of their own, in the same lamentable position.

The Governor has travelled around the Island to see things, and perhaps to do things. He has seen with his eyes the people in their Sunday dresses, but Executives are required to visualize conditions beyond the sight of the eyes. If he has done this, can you tell me, Mr. Editor, how could he be adding up 400% more tax than what the people used to pay? Haven't we got enough bankruptcy in this country? Are the people not shuddering enough from hunger? Is the Government so blind as not to see that the unhappy ones are returning to the state from how they came to this world - nude? Does not the Government understand that extra tax will only tend to increase Governmental situations? Must I ask if the Government has no respect for the feelings of the poor, and no regard whatever for their happiness?

Hundreds of thousands of Pounds should be used on Agriculture so that we should get financial returns in the years to come. We have heard nothing of that, but we hear that gold is to be sunk in some of the harbours of the Island.

Mr. Editor, I cannot intrude any further on your generosity, but I must conclude in saying that the whole matter looks to me that the business of the island and the welfare of the people have been thrown into the hands of unbusiness-like people. Can there be a greater calamity? Than even the Ethiopian War! And what shall we do? What can we do? We can only wait and expect all nights in the country.

This extra taxation and the ungodly suggestions as to how the money is to be spent at this time, is a moral crime.

It is to be fully understood that when I say Government, I am not including the majority of the Elected Members, most of whom are doing their best by protecting us against the unheard of rise of taxation at such a time as this.

I am etc.,
Alexander Bustamante,
la Duke Street,
Kingston,
October 18, 1935.

THE SEVEN SIGNERS

THE EDITOR,

Sir,

I begin by saying with every sincerity that without a paper like yours, which impartially publishes the views of all, this country would be a terrible place to live in. In fact, I personally would have a desire to walk out of this Island by foot.

I am in a position to state that your paper equals the best I have read in any part of the world - whether it has one million inhabitants, or 150 millions, and I have had the pleasure of knowing dozens of countries.

With regard to the letter by the Member for Manchester, which appeared in your column recently, I definitely feel that he would have gained respect if he faced facts and admitted his error even by saying that the Government caught me in a weak moment, and that's the reason why I submitted to the threat, "No taxation, no loan", and gave my word to vote for taxation.

It is a strong man who apologises for his wrong, it is weakness to cover up. And this gentleman concludes in saying - "I feel sure, Mr. Editor, if you are engaged in a fight with another man and your opponent has cause to surrender and accordingly does so, you would not be so cowardly to continue hitting him. Why expect it of us?"

Will Mr. Reid tell me how and in what way did the Government surrender, and if the Government did surrender, as is implied in his last paragraph, why did six or seven of them have to pledge to the Government, to raise taxes and to make this promise into a verbal contract, why one of their number elected to act as spokesman to publish this verbal contract?

Mr. Reid's last paragraph is a Japanese puzzle, for the public is convinced of one fact to their detriment, that seven men surrendered, unjustly so to their discredit. It would seem that Mr. Reid's intention is to strike us with the same tactic as the Government used upon them. Personally, Mr. Reid's diplomacy, if we should call it that, cannot change facts, and I boldly say that there is not one man in the Government from the Captain at the helm of our ship down, who could make a school boy out of me and get me to act in an unbusiness-like fashion or against the interest of the people. This is just what the Government has done to the seven Legislators, and if what I say here hurt anyone, may it become a permanent wound in their minds so that childish action might not be repeated, and I have no apology to offer as a balm for such wounds.

I have kindly feeling to a couple of the Legislators who submitted to the Government, but if they chose to be narrow-minded enough to allow this letter to serve as a division between our friendship, it's their privilege.

I have heard Legislators say that the reason why they cannot get better advantage in the Legislative Council is owing to the very limited power they have under our Constitution. I say this is not true, and I am emphasising upon the absurdity of such an assertion. I say without fear, that it is not the Constitution which is hopelessly imbecile.

I think Shakespeare once wrote: "It's a wise man who knows when to stop speaking." It is also said that Caesar was murdered for the good of the state.

Disaster is facing us - not through our Constitution, but through most of the Elected Members. It would seem to me that instead of the people of this island being blest with the right kind of people to represent them, we are being suffocated by most of them.

There is a previous letter in your office regarding this same matter, and I must now ask you for the sake of the interest of the people to do as you have always done, spare me a little space and publish it also.

We cannot allow the Member from Manchester to "soft-soap" us with a little letter which does not merit consideration. All the Legislators are of adult age, but some of them are too young as Legislators, not in age of course. Their youthfulness is causing gray hair even in young tax-payers through worries and unless we expose their youthfulness to the public with the hope that they will grow up in a business-like manner, the majority of us will be like a baldplate in its second year, with white head, or like a vulture - no hair on the head.

One listens to some of them speaking and can easily detect that although they can make links they cannot form them into chains. Just how your reporters are able to furnish speeches in such a clarified way is a mystery to the writer. I can only come to one conclusion, that your Paper possesses some of the most intelligent reporters, as any other Paper I have known.

Many of the Legislators we may call new. It is a pity we have to pay for the experience of some, for I would think that they would prepare themselves for such an important office before they would dare to betray the people by asking them for their votes. If they would only stop to think that they needed other qualifications beside street-box or hill-side oratory, courage would fail them to do so. More unfortunate is the fact that some of the veteran Legislators who could really serve the people if they wanted to, are just as bad, in fact worse, for it is not for the lack of their not knowing what to do and how to do it. You can therefore see that the Legislative Council is, today, composed, in a great part, of mysteries and disaster. They are a few who are doing well, you can count them upon your four fingers. You may laugh, you may cry, you can term me foolish, but I tell you again, fellow-citizens, that the day we lose J.A.G. Smith, K.C., out of the Council, it will be a sorrowful loss to this Island.

Man must die, that is the law of God, over which we have no control, but it is a sad thing that every man must die.

Again I am thanking you, Mr. Editor, in advance for publishing this letter.

I am etc.,
Alexander Bustamante,
1a Duke Street,
Kingston,
November 10,1935.

INCIDENT IN COUNCIL

THE EDITOR,

Sir,

In reference to my letter in your paper, in which I stated that the Governor ordered the Member for St. Mary when he was speaking upon a subject that was being discussed in the Legislative Council, to sit down, I noticed in the Gleaner recently wherein Mr. Vernon, referring to my statement, wrote: "I am bound to say that in fair play to all concerned it is incorrect. The Governor did not, could not, and will not at any time be able to tell me to take my seat, for the reason that I was not on the occasion mentioned by Mr. Bustamante, drunk, rude, or out of order."

Mr. Editor, I am sorry that Mr. Vernon possesses that strange courage of contradicting an absolute fact; more sorry am I, because Mr. Vernon is one of the very first men I met when I returned to this country a couple of years ago, and in fact I considered him a friend.

Before I penned the letter which Mr. Vernon referred to, I recalled our acquaintance. Of course, in public life I cannot and will not be influenced by anything but the truth and fact. I must again confirm that it is definitely true that whilst Mr. Vernon was speaking on a subject under consideration in the Legislative Council, the Governor imperatively ordered him to sit down. The Governor's order was so pronounced, that although I was not the person addressed, I felt it. It is an absolute fact that Mr. Vernon weakly retorted to the Governor:"I did not know you could do that", (meaning "to order me to sit down"). The Governor replied, "Yes, I can", and Mr. Vernon then sunk into his seat as if he were lifeless, which made me feel like a Turkish Bath hot and cold, at the lack of spirit for self-defence.

The Hon. J.A.G. Smith, K.C., came in about three minutes before the incident, and took up a defensive attitude towards Mr. Vernon, and told him he had a right to speak.

In the letter of Mr. Vernon in question, he writes: "The Governor will not at any time be able to order me to take my seat for the reason that I was not on the occasion mentioned by Mr. Bustamante drunk, etc.,", I know Mr. Vernon as a sober person, not alone on that occasion but on every and all occasions I have seen him. But when he writes as he has written, "will not at anytime order me to take my seat", he must have meant that the Governor will not duplicate his order, and if Mr. Vernon pretends that he knows what the Governor will do, then I can only compare his wisdom with that of Solomon's.

In referring to the Governor in the last paragraph of his letter, Mr. Vernon writes - "It's human to err, and whilst I am not going to say the Governor is free of mistakes, I honestly believe that he has the best interests of the Island at heart." I will not state that the Hon. Member is not correct in that, for I agree that the Governor is badly advised.

I am against encouraging children who continually commit unwise acts, then how foolish would I be or anyone else for that much, not to criticise the action of this Governor and his Government.

I say as I have said already, that it is one thing to perform soap-box oration to obtain votes. This does not need so much skill in this country, for the people forgot so often of the baits that have been thrown out in the past, and although they have been caught by them, they still allow themselves to be caught by even bare hooks without any food upon them, and that is why some of these aimless, meaningless Legislators have again caught our people to the detriment of our country.

We would be better off without most of our present Legislators.

£35,000 I understand have been put aside to build a new Legislative House. I wonder if a little room in the Governor's house would not be a little more suitable so that the Governor might have them not alone under his thumb, but under his eyes.

I feel that Mr. Vernon would co-operate with the Governor for the best of our country, for I honestly believe that he is with the people and for the people, but rulers - I say rulers, not Governors, do not invite co-operation, they order as now Mr. Vernon was ordered down. Then how can Mr. Vernon co-operate for the greatest good for the greatest number. The expression "the greatest good for the greatest number" might be true in the Corporation Council, but it does not apply to the Legislative Council.

Mr. Vernon is not in accordance with the harsh treatment levelled against His Execellency by destructive critics. May I ask Mr. Vernon if he too is helping to deceive the public for when he says "destructive critics" it is an implication that the greater number of us Jamaicans who are criticising the Governor and his Government are doing so deliberately which means that we are deceiving our people. I personally have no axe to grind out of the Government and that is the reason why I can criticise freely.

I am etc.,
Alexander Bustamante,
1a Duke Street,
Kingston.
November 25, 1935.

BATHLESS HOUSES
Mr. Bustamante and His Critics

THE EDITOR,

Sir,

I am craving your indulgence for entering again the arena of Bathless houses in Jamaica, Jim Crow Cars in America, and Jim Crow Hotels in England chiefly from the fact that "Ginger" is attacking me from many corners, even from the rear.

In the issue of your weekly contemporary of the 7th inst., "Ginger" wrote: "Mr. Alex Bustamante has let loose his heavy Artillery against me both in the 'Jamaica Times' of the 23rd November, and in the 'Daily Gleaner' of the 25th, and his letters are a fair sample of newspaper correspondence in Jamaica, for he omits some vital parts of what I wrote and accuses me of silly statements, etc.,".

I am positive that ninety-five percent of your readers have already agreed with me that it was a very silly thing for "Ginger" to say that "it was within living memory that the better classes in America ever bathed at all." Such a statement would be just as silly as if it were said against any other civilized country.

In "Ginger's" letter of the 7th inst., he said that he did not mean Americans in particular; he could have said the same against any other northern country and it would have been equally true. I say that every intelligent person would know it is equally untrue. But how could I have known that "Ginger" didn't really mean Americans in particular, when I had never pretended to be a telepathist like Professor Zander?

Continuing, "Ginger" says that I am the ignorant one, for I did not do him the honour of reading all he wrote, otherwise I never would have said "Ginger, you have made a statement that not a single person besides you have ever heard or known of." Yes, "Ginger", I have read all of your letter of November 16, and the whole country is laughing at your statement that "it is within living memory that the better classes of America ever bathed at all." Instead of apologising for this truthless statement, you have made a meaningless attempt in your letter of the 7th inst., to offer an excuse for your blunder, which is nothing else but a feeble and picturesque after-thought on your part. You are only making a vile attempt to make yourself more conspicuous.

You have accused me of side-tracking important statements which you made on the 16th inst., and which you quoted from Sir Wm. Butler's book, where he says that if there had been an eleventh commandment in America (1870 or thereby) it would have been: "Thou shalt not tub" and that one American wrote in the "Saturday Evening Post" that America gave the bath tub to the world. Those myths are the important things that you want the public to believe that I side-tracked, because I did not want to face their issues.

They were not deserving of any comment from me, because they are just fantasies with which you filled up your letter, evidently for not having anything more interesting in your mind at that time of writing.

It is very obvious that your letter of the 7th inst., was impelled through the desire of wanting to wriggle out of a statement which lacks the spice of veracity.

"Ginger" stated in his letter of the 7th inst., that some people who expected to be in London advertised for a flat and in finding one, found that although this flat was not yet unoccupied, the bath was inhabited by coals, and the out-going lady explained that they did not use it. All the quotations you have made about houses having fixed baths and coal in baths, might be very interesting and even amusing, but does not help to prove your statement that within living memory the better classes of America did not bathe at all. You have reminded me of the cunning fox penned up in an iron cage and vainly trying to break through.

Anyone who wants to know about the Jim Crow Hotels in London can test the veracity of my statement by writing to some official of the League of Coloured People. It does not matter whether it is in the street cars of Southern America, or in the Hotels of England, when they do not want the Negroes or the very dark people to associate with the whites in the same car or Hotel. Both are termed Unwritten Jim Crow Law. You are a great person in trying to wriggle out of known facts, but I have got you so well lassoed that there is no possible way for you to make an honourable escape, unless you are going to use your teeth to cut loose the rope.

"Ginger" would like to ask Mr. T.S. Phillips, late Editor of the 'Jamaica Times', how he was received in England. "Ginger", I look upon that suggestion from you as very unkind to me because for me to get the history of Mr. Phillips' treatment in England, I would have to ask him some very pointed and pertinent questions. Mr. Phillips would then smite me with his facile pen for my impertinence, and poor defenceless me, would have to take the count as "Ginger" is now taking it, and it would be all due to his unconsidered advice to me. I would no doubt make myself his enemy, so, I do not think much of you as a Counsel, "Ginger".

There is another phase to this Comedy of Errors, Mr. Editor. "Pro Bono Publico" recently wrote in your "Daily Gleaner" that "Ginger" was absolutely correct when he stated that Americans are reluctant in bathing but "Ginger" in his letter of the 7th inst., says that it wasn't really America he was thinking of when he wrote about bathless Americans. The whole affair looks to me like a tragedy for "Ginger" and his defenders. I feel sure, therefore, that "Pro Bono Publico" has now disrobed himself of his bull-fighting costume.

This comedy has now developed into a triangle for R.S. Murray writing in the "Gleaner" from Frankfield P.O. on the 5th inst., said he would not pose as "Ginger's" champion. I want to say that a cowardly man keeps sound bones and I admire this sense of self-protection as shown by Mr. Murray. But Mr. Murray did say that it is the height of bad manners on my part to have said in respect of "Ginger" that "head stays and mind becomes foggy".

Mr. Editor, please allow me to ask Mr. Murray, how does he measure the height of bad manners? Is it with a tape measure or with a yard stick? And unless he can enlighten me on the point I shall refuse to accept his admonition.

A monument of these two unofficial historians - "Ginger" and "Pro Bono Publico" will one day, I hope, stand side by side, hand in hand on the waterfront of Kingston with Mr. Murray kneeling before them with hands clasped, head uplifted toward heaven, imploring the blessing of God so that their souls may be cleansed in this sinful history of Bathless Americans.

I am etc.,
Alexander Bustamante,
1a Duke Street,
Kingston,
December 10, 1935.

COUNCIL INCIDENT
Mr. Bustamante and the Elected Members

THE EDITOR,

Sir,

In response to Mr. H.E. Vernon's letter in your issue of even date, I must say that he has again strayed from the truth when he states that he was not ordered to take his seat, whilst speaking upon a subject in the Legislative Council. In furthering his denial in this matter, he said that the Governor of this country is a gentleman of refinement and would never place himself in the unfortunate position of creating a scene in Council by ordering members of that body to take their seats when not guilty of any irregularity.

In reference to the Governor's gentility, I would go further than Mr. Vernon, by adding that the Governor possesses a pleasing and charming personality. But many of these crouching and unimpressive legislators do not demand the respect of the Governor.

I notice that since I wrote the first letter regarding this matter, Mr. Vernon has shown a stronger courage in the Council and that was the result I aimed at that my letter should accomplish and so I think I am well rewarded for being termed mischievous.

In regard to the Governor not placing himself in the unfortunate position to create a scene in Council by ordering members to sit down when not guilty of any irregularity; well, a scene was created in truth, for the Hon. J.A.G. Smith, K.C., demonstrated his indignation on the imposition on the Hon. Member of St. Mary's right, so much so that Mr. Smith told Mr. Vernon that he had a right to speak. The Governor then said to Mr. Smith, "Please".

Mr. Smith then got up and spoke and among other things he said: "I am not going to accept any insult from this part or that part, or no part of this House." Then, how on earth can Mr. Vernon dare to contradict a naked truth?

It is certainly a known fact that there is no unity between the Elected Members; that on occasions when the Governor calls them to order through Parliamentary regulation or otherwise, the Elected Members actually jeered and laughed at each other. There is as much unity between them as shredded wheat and its chaff, and that is one of the reasons why our country is not progressing.

The majority of the Elected Members show no feeling of defence towards their constituents, none whatever between themselves and that is one of the chief reasons why this Government has been able to go contrary to the principles of British justice, by making bad laws, and our country will no doubt get worse as the night cedes into day until our people are educated enough to choose men of independent minds, men who will not be dominated by social hypocrisy.

We must elect men who do not alone realize that we are a subject people and that Governors are sent here, not because they are better than us, but because we must have an Administrator, and that we must give him the respect he deserves, but we need not feel and look upon him with any feeling of inferiority.

Some time ago I noticed in the "Gleaner" written by a gentleman from St. Thomas in which he urged that in order to get better legislators, there should be a requirement of £1,200 clear annual income of candidates aspiring for election to Council. I cannot agree with this, because one's earning is no guarantee for his honesty or dishonesty. We, therefore, want to select men for their intelligence and honour, men of independent minds and integrity, partiots who will think of the public and not merely of themselves, men who will realise that social hypocrisy is a danger to civilization and damaging to the State.

We have a few older men in the Council who possess all the qualifications of Statesmen as far as the requirements of this country are concerned. What have they done for the State and the people since the present sitting of the Legislative Counicl? Nothing. And why have they not done anything worthwhile? What is the influence operating (if any)? Shall we ever forget that Match Bill, when nearly all the Elected Members allowed the Government to infringe upon our rights without saying one word in our favour? The conscience of these men must have been like an active volcano within them - tearing them apart. What was the cause of the silence of their voices?

The Banana Bill is too fresh for the most shallow mind to be forgotten. It is my duty towards my country and my people to expose these bad laws and the actions of our Legislators before the public, not alone yesterday, nor to-day, but to-morrow. They are at liberty to say what they may of me - even of being mischievous, etc., but nothing they can say will silence me; nothing they can do will hurt me; but they are hurting my people - the masses of this Island, and until there is an amelioration of these conditions I shall continue to expose them.

Mr. Vernon having contradicted a naked truth, is another proof of the weakness of most of our Legislators. What has become of the wise men of our country?

The men of our country are failing us, and I am strongly suggesting that our women should come forward in public life and replace weak-kneed men. With that inner courage possessed by women combined with their intuition and with a sense of more truth than men, I believe that they would help to mould the character of the men to be more useful. Men might them become ashamed and redeem themselves back to honour and respect.

I am etc.,
Alexander Bustamante,
1a Duke Street,
Kingston,
December 11, 1935.

"BATHLESS AMERICANS"?

THE EDITOR,

Sir,

In the "Gleaner" of today "Ginger" quoted Mr. Vernon Fung of 130 Church Street as saying that "Ginger's" contention is — "that the Americans very seldom take a bath".

"Will he, or anyone else, tell me when I, by word of mouth or in print, ever said so?" This is the question "Ginger" has asked.

"Ginger", you have never put such a statement in print; if you did so by word of mouth I did not hear you.

The following is the statement you put in print, "Ginger" — "It is within living memory that only the better classes in America — Doctors, Lawyers, etc., bathed at all." That is the identical statement you made — and much worse than Mr. Fung's statement, and because I remarked — "Ginger", you are the only one who knows or ever heard of such an absurdity, and that head stays and mind fogs, etc.," you said that I was personal. Then you tried to let the public believe me in the weekly publication of the 21st inst., that I made those remarks because you said "comparisons are odious" and in spite of my becoming personal "I suppose I still will have to call Mr. Bustamante a gentleman".

Now "Ginger", I am strongly suggesting to you that you must never try again to contradict your own statement. It is not nice. Please turn a new leaf for the New Year, repent and re-born, otherwise you might never reach the Kingdom of Heaven owing to the unheard of statement you wrote of "Bathless Americans".

Good luck and good health for the New Year, "Ginger", and more sane thinking.

I am etc.,
Alexander Bustamante,
1a Duke Street,
Kingston,
December 23, 1935.

BATHLESS HOUSES
APOLOGIES

THE EDITOR,

Sir,

It takes a broad mind and a big heart to apologise for one's error, whether the error was made consciously or unconsciously. I must, therefore, thank "Ginger" through your press, for his apology to me in your Editorial page of even date, that it was not true that your weekly contemporary had ever refused to publish any letters from me.

In the said letter under review "Ginger" confirmed his first letter in the "Jamaica Times" that it is true that he himself wrote — "It is within living memory that Americans hardly ever bathed at all", and that in truth and in fact he had never contradicted the above, and that he now asks me for an apology for my having stated that he did contradict the said statement.

It is a fact that I wrote "Ginger" contradicted his own statement. I did so, because that is what I believe I saw penned by him. However, as "Ginger" has now written that he had never contradicted his statement, I feel that I am in honour bound to ask "Ginger" to accept my apology for making a statement which he said is incorrect.

I am etc.,
Alexander Bustamante,
1a Duke Street,
Kingston,
January 10, 1936.

CONDITIONS IN JAMAICA

THE EDITOR,

Sir,

Why are foreign Bands allowed to perform in this Island when there are hundreds, if not a thousand native musicians unemployed here?

Positions that Jamaicans can fill, people are brought from over the ocean to deprive them of. This is very pronounced in the Police Force.

Is our paternal father only supposed to whip us when we do not obey and not to protect us when we need protection?

I am not blaming his Excellency Governor Denham alone, for inadequate protection of our interests, but Elected Members are chiefly the ones who are bringing to this Island more sorrow, thinking not of the people whose only hope seem to be the ending of their last days in Government institutions.

The invasion of people from over the ocean to take out of our people's mouths that which they are dying for — bread, is a lack of wisdom on the part of the Government.

Will the Government continue closing its eyes against this foreign invasion? We must demand protection from the Government.

I am etc.,
Alexander Bustamante,
1a Duke Street,
Kingston,
January 13,1936.

THE LATE KING GEORGE V.

THE EDITOR,

Sir,

Whilst we mourn the loss of our late King George V, he is resting in peace — perfect peace, in the arms of Christ, I believe. He has gained the greatest of reward — the Kingdom of heaven, I feel. Then indeed in the midst of sorrow what greater consolation can we have for the loss of our loved King than the belief that his soul is resting in the Kingdom of the mightiest Kingdoms — heaven; that he is now with the mightiest of Kings, the only perfect King — God our Heavenly Father.

His earthly loss to us means a heavenly gain to Him, I believe; then in the midst of sorrow and the shedding of tears, we should rejoice at the belief that he has gained that which all men should strive and work for — the salvation of the soul.

I think not of him alone as a King, but a man beloved by his subjects — by his people; beloved and respected by the entire universe — not through his once mighty, earthly power, but for his just ways, not alone to the strong, but to the weak, to all.

Again what a consolation to be able to say that our late King was a good King — the popular King. We have lots to be grateful to God for, sufficient to soothe our sorrow for his great loss.

He lived not for himself and his Royal people; he was unselfish, he lived for all. His entire and exemplary life was like that of an angel watching over his people and praying for the good of mankind.

Some 35 years ago, the late Queen Victoria of blessed memory departed from this world to the Beyond. The entire world then mourned her loss; even the skies; it was man's heart saddened by her departure from this world.

History has once more repeated itself. The hearts of men today are filled with sorrow. The skies seem to be in sympathy with our sad feeling for the departure of our late King from this life. The rain which we had yesterday, after long absence of that blessing, seems to confirm my feeling. Long live the new King.

I am etc.,
Alexander Bustamante,
1a Duke Street,
Kingston,
January 24, 1936.

OUR WOMEN DEFENDED

THE EDITOR,

Sir,

I have seen much nonsense written by newspaper correspondents, but I do not remember seeing more slotted nonsense written than by "A Stranger Within The Gate" in the Pink Sheet of your Journal of the 1st inst. Your correspondent tried to be comical in his leading paragraph, but his little attempt fades into senselessness.

He attacks the morals of our women - that girls who should know better would go on ships to make acquaintance with men, and that they will call men up whom they have never known or never met and invite them to come to their homes, to take them out.

No well-thinking persons who know our girls would believe this contemptible untruth. This man must have come across those who have sunken into degradation through poverty or otherwise, and cannot distinguish them from the flower of our womanhood. He would not dare to make such a statement of womanhood in my adopted country, Spain, and get away with it.

Your correspondent continues to say that girls who park at Rockfort late at nights make it their point of duty to find out occupants of other cars. I do not park anywhere, so I do not know. However, throughout the world it is the business of women to find the business of others; and that "they know the business of even the fifth generation of each other." This, of course, might be true, for this is a small land; but what makes my blood boil is that he has the effrontery, the audacity and the impudence to infer that our girls, who should know better, are hunting down strange men on ships and streets, and that classes in Jamaica appear to be undistinguished by difference in moral code.

In the last paragraph of your correspondent's communication he wrote:- "One of the most striking things in this country is the absence of good manners. People are not courteous to each other; social manners in men seem to be non-existent. One never sees the man who stands at the approach of a lady or jumps up quickly to fetch a chair or to draw her chair when sitting or rising."

In this I definitely agree with "The Stranger Within The Gate", and I take it for granted why this man has observed so keenly this fact is because he might be from a northern land where courtesy and hospitality is extended to women of all walks of life. This is also the custom of Latin countries. Of course, I know that the writer of that article is not Latin, because the Latins possess the greatest regard for womanhood. In spite of their temperamental nature, they are kind in words and deeds to their women except when there might be cause for jealousy, then she must expect to pay. There is not the slightest doubt that discourtesy of all kinds is rampant in this country. Men are definitely not courteous to women in this country and this applies to all walks of life. As a matter of fact, courtesy is very lacking here with both men and women alike. There are exceptions, of course, and I conscientiously say that one of these exceptions is to be found in the Editorial Department of the Gleaner. When one has lived out of this Island, as I have, it is easy to appreciate courtesy and it is just as easy to detect discourtesy.

I personally do not think that within the hearts of Jamaicans the feeling of discourtesy exists but they do not know how to accompany hospitality with courtesy, and I repeat that I agree with "The Stranger Within The Gate" that discourtesy is rampant in this Island. It is bad among the women, it is worse among the men.

We lack badly that Northern and Latin hospitality — we lack that thing which costs nothing – courtesy.

I am etc.,
Alexander Bustamante,
1a Duke Street,
Kingston,
February 3, 1936.

EDITORIAL ARTICLE CRITICISED

THE EDITOR,

Sir,

In entering the playground of a lion, one must think of consequences, and as I am about to cross the path of the Editor of this paper, I think of the cunning yet silly fox trying to enter the cage of a prancing tiger. Personally, I have contempt for fear and danger, therefore I am never afraid to tread upon the most dangerous ground, as my mind is always made up to accept and bear consequences.

In your issue of even date, you have given great prominence to the effect that "one of the ablest men in all the West Indies - whether British or otherwise, and himself a Jamaican, mentioned to us yesterday that the question of suitable sites for T.B. Hospitals has been thoroughly discussed in England some time ago, and not merely among Doctors and in the Press, but also in the House of Commons and the House of Lords. He informed us that the investigation in England had demonstrated that a T.B. Hospital, even in a crowded area, was no danger whatever to the people living in the vicinity."

However, the main factor is, that although eminent Doctors, and in fact every Doctor taught us that T.B. is a very contagious disease, the House of Lords and Commons and Doctors still say that a T.B. Hospital can be placed in the midst of the thickest population without the slightest risk, even the unwise can readily see that both teachings conflict, and in spite of the decision of the Houses of Lords and Commons and their Doctors, there is not one country that I know of (and I know dozens) that are to-day building T.B. Sanatoriums, in or around the Cities.

You will find in England itself that sanatoriums are scattered in isolated places. Why is this done then if the cities are just as suitable places for them? Why throughout the length and breadth of the United States of America they are flung in isolated spots amongst hills, mountains and pine walks? Why is it, if the cities are proper places for such an institution that those who are kept in such institutions in the cities temporarily are transferred to sanatoriums in the country as soon as vacancies occur?

Your Editorial might influence those who have not read or have not travelled as it has influenced many with the Beacon Match Bill, (I will be told there is no such Bill) but a bean is a bean no matter what other name you may give it; but it will not influence the other section of the community who have read, much more those who have seen how sanatoriums are placed where sanitation is considered very good.

Within the last year in this country, the people have not been swallowing Editorials unchewed, but they have been re-chewing them. This fact I am sure, you, Mr. Editor, have realised. The people have become awakened to injustices and today are like a thoroughbred horse, ready for action. We are not prepared to swallow the opinions of a couple Government advisors without thinking for ourselves. There are a few men in this country today (I am one of them) who are ready and willing at all times to stand by the side of justice and fair play.

Your Editorial in question is written in a manner tending to influence the public against their own interests in favour of the opinion of the Superintendent Medical Officer. As Mr. Smith truly wrote, a few will soon leave the Island, whilst we Jamaicans must stay here and burn. I will always say that the kind of men we want in this country are men of Mr. Smith's calibre — men who have no fear and men who are not seeking Knighthoods. One of the things that is ruining us here is this vain title we all want, and after we have obtained it, we are still commoners.

Can you tell me, Mr. Editor, of even one country where a T.B. Sanatorium is placed in the vicinity of an open reservoir? "We have been reminded also that just outside of Havana stands the T.B. Sanatorium of that city and in the neighbourhood of plenty of residents who are not affected either physically or emotionally by this proximity." Did you ask your informer if he had taken an X-Ray picture of the inhabitants of that locality, or did he go around with an emotional machine registering emotions? Or does it mean that if in Havana, horses are ridden with the rider's face towards the tail that we should do the same here? Can't you see, Mr. Editor, that you have not put forth one desirability whatever regarding the placing of this Sanatorium at Mona that could influence the intelligent public?

"The T.B. germs also, are not mosquitoes that fly around." That is what you have penned. Well, well, Mr. Editor, we are very grateful to you for such information, but the fact is well known. However, the germs can be borne by wind in dust or carried by flies and other insects from the sputum of the diseased persons to infest others at a distance.

I am sure that every person who has protested against this, and all those who feel that Mona is not the right place for the Sanatorium, but have remained silent, are heartily sorry that the occasion should have arisen to make it necessary for them to enter their protests, because we are deeply sorry for those who are suffering from this unfortunate disease; but it is just as much for their safety as well as for the benefit of others, why the sanatorium should be placed in a different locality, where the focus of infection could be circumscribed and effectively dealt with.

"Certainly it could not constitute anything like the risk run by those people who built towns on the slopes of an active volcano in Italy or Central America." Now, Mr. Editor, you are straying from the subject altogether. What has that got to do with this matter in question? Because I might be silly enough to sit on the edge of a keg of gun-powder, is that any reason why we should fly in the face of Providence and build the sanatorium on the proposed site?

You conclude that "unless a sort of panic unfortunately prevails...." Let me assure you, Mr. Editor, that there is a panic and justifiably so, and it is "the sincere wish that there should very speedily be a reasonable determination arrived at in regard to the proposed site of the T.B. Sanatorium."

I am etc.,
Alexander Bustamante,
1a Duke Street,
Kingston,
February 11, 1936.

SITE FOR T.B. SANATORIUM CRITICISED

THE EDITOR,

Sir,

Some time ago a doctor wrote that Wareika Hill is a suitable place for the erection of a T.B. Sanatorium for it would be in easy access. I sympathise with the innocent knowledge of the doctor regarding this matter. I presume that Kingston is not the only place that contains T.B. then indeed it would not be convenient for outdoor patients from Hanover and other distant places.

Besides it is a known fact that in other known countries where things are done in a more orderly manner than here, an infectious and contagious disease hospital near cities is not in the interest of visitors and patients because it is not desirable to have visitors to flock there in abundance on every visiting day and as to getting doctors in case of emergency; this is ridiculous, because the hospital should have a permanent staff to take care of all and every such case.

Eight miles from Montreal, one hundred and fifty miles from Madrid and on an island in New York are where contagious hospitals are located. That is an act of civilization and we should imitate those whose actions show that they know more than us.

Wareika Hill is desirable from only one angle and that is the height. It is undesirable for any other requirement; it is within close proximity of many populous districts, too close to Rock Spring water supply. Sanitary pits must be of necessity sunken on the hill and no man can say how far the refuse will penetrate, it might penetrate as far down to the source from which the well receives its water supply, which means that the well might be contaminated from these pits; also from the air. Then again, has it ever dawned on people that the death rate of consumptives is extremely high? Have they ever stopped to think that the procession of these corpses must flow down from Wareika Hill and then through some part of the Corporate Area to further tax the mind of our unfortunate people and tourists and to leave a sad impression upon our youngsters who of necessity must come in contact with this affair? The whole thing is pathetic and how such an idea could have emanated from the brains of anyone who lays claim to intelligence or to anything that savours to it is beyond my comprehension.

I am sorry that I should have to write on this subject for my heart goes out to the unfortunates who are victims of this dreaded disease. They too have loved ones and they might think that it is through scorn that we are insisting that this hospital should not be put at Mona or Wareika Hill. This is not the case: it is only through the sympathy we have for them and for the safety of those more fortunate why we are insisting that Government act more wisely, otherwise we might have to build more sanatoriums. Fellow citizens, wouldn't that be serious—wouldn't that be very sad? Then indeed we must call upon everyone irrespective of class or creed to extend their voices against this proposal.

The writer is now making a personal appeal to the Governor of this Colony to put the health of the people above all and everything else. When I say the people, I refer also to the victims of T.B. because it is not alone to the interest of the sick that they should recover rapidly, but also to the financial interest of the Government and rapid recovery can only be obtained through the most ideal climate that Jamaica possesses and a proper diet. Such a locality cannot be found in close proximity to the Corporate Area. Then as Santa Cruz and Malvern are the most suitable places, why not locate it there?

In conclusion, if the Government insist in using its power and treating the voice of the majority with contempt, then I strongly suggest that public meetings should be held to protest. I volunteer my service as a speaker.

I am etc.,
Alexander Bustamante,
1a Duke Street,
Kingston,
March 9, 1936.

OF THE JAMAICAN WOMAN AND SPORTS

THE EDITOR,

Sir,

Women of this Island do not take sufficient active interest in sports. There is but one reason and that is there are too many social classes in this island; every shade of complexion, and almost every different financial position means a different class socially.

The woman or man who can drive a motorcar whether they can afford it or not (and most of them cannot afford it) is higher than his or her sister who walks the street for necessity or who would rather do so in preference of having nightmares and even day-dreams as to where the installment is coming from. One can clearly see the reason why there is so much lack of love and unity among us, and the reason why women take so little interest in active sports. This does not apply only to women but even to men with their foolish class distinction — a distinction which is self-centered — a distinction which prevents progress and the building of healthier bodies in men and women, and when one stops to think that nine-tenths of the people of this country are mixed with the same white and African blood, one cannot but feel the narrow-mindedness of our country men and women. Many will frown at this letter, but they can sneer all they want to, this is a fact which cannot be truly denied. We should leave social standing for our drawing rooms, and not bring it so prominently into sport.

In many countries that can be termed a white population you will invariably find classes of different kind entering the same sport. Why? Because it is meant not just for beauty building but for health and a charming disposition and tend to produce healthy mothers. Then why should not all respectable people compete irrespective of race, creed or nationality?

Sometimes, a dark girl might be more intelligent and of higher social standing than her fairer sister, but owing to her dark pigment, her fairer sister does not want to enter the same sport as she is in. Then it is really on account of her darker skin, or is it because her fairer sisters envy her beauty?

One can see amongst the poorest peasants some of the most beautifully formed women in Jamaica, but I suppose that the girl of higher social standing would hate to know that this dark peasant was judged the most beautiful bathing beauty. Then perhaps it is not really social standing why so many of the so-called better social women of this island refuse to enter beauty contests, but they are afraid and perhaps ashamed that many of their inferior sisters are more beautiful than they are. It is time and time past for us to stop refusing to enter sports, because we are so self-centered to believe that we are better than others. This feeling is generally a mental one which disgusts many who have no such mental affection and therefore think differently.

The people of this island, in general, put me in mind of little towns where the side-walks are taken in at 7 o'clock at nights and the inhabitants peeping through their windows looking at their neighbours to see what might be found to gossip about.

In conclusion, sports is made as an inducement, not alone for beautiful forms but to benefit the body, the mind, the soul and to reproduce better and healthier people and to reduce the discomforts of motherhood. So class prejudice should be smashed to earth, to ashes, for the betterment of the people, so as to create a healthier people, and more cheerful minds mean a better country, then why so much class-distinction in sports? Leave that distinction for your drawing room, enter sports and compete, forget this foolish class distinction which neither takes you here nor there, up or down, but makes you appear ridiculous in the sight of the broadminded and well-thinking people.

I am etc.,
Alexander Bustamante,
1a Duke Street,
Kingston,
July 4, 1936.

THE J.P.S. AND MONOPOLY

THE EDITOR,

Sir,

I noticed in your journal that the Jamaica Public Service want to monopolise the Corporate Area bus service. One would think that this company would first learn to operate a proper trolley-car service before they should assume such an aspiration. One would also think that the company would not run a one-man car as a proof to us that they have an interest in the country and people in reducing unemployment. This same company has the monopoly of the lighting system; they charge such high prices that I have never seen or heard of until I came to this country. Why? Because there is no competition?

We have been driven out of the grocery business, the dry goods, and we are being driven out of the produce. Strangers are even taking away the truckman's job. There is strong opposition against us in the spirit business and now they want to drive us out of the transportation system.

We are going to fight this to the bitter end, and we are looking forward to the captain of the helm of this ship for justice and protection. Can't you see that the big man is trying to drive the small man to a state of desperation?

The bus owners of this country are the true children of the soil. Their systems of operation is not perfect now, but each day it is improving. Nevertheless, it is more perfect than the trolley-car system and furthermore, they employ two persons to run one bus while the Public Service Company employs one man to be motorman and conductor.

I realise the Governor will be given the same kind of insincere advice as is the custom in this island; so that the big man should become bigger financially thus impoverishing the small man more and more, but the Governor has been with us for nearly two years now and will think for himself instead of taking everything for granted. I am not against the P.S.Co., and I think the trolley-car service should continue to exist, but they must not be allowed to monopolise the transport system.

I am etc.,
Alexander Bustamante,
1a Duke Street,
Kingston,
July 6, 1936.

BEE INSTRUCTOR

THE EDITOR,

Sir,

I should be much obliged if you would be kind enough to publish the following letter to the members of the Jamaica Agricultural Society as early as you can.

1a Duke Street,
Kingston,
August 3, 1936.

THE MEMBERS OF THE JAMAICA AGRICULTURAL SOCIETY:

Ladies and gentlemen, I desire to bring to your attention the position which has arisen in regard to the appointment of Mr. H. H. Coote as Bee Instructor.

As each day passes without any decisive action in the matter, it becomes abundantly clear that a determined stand is being made against Mr. Coote. It would appear that the Hon. Director of Agriculture has made up his mind to enforce his will upon the Board of Management despite the fact that no charges have ever been proven against this unfortunate man, Mr. Coote, and that the bee-keepers of the island are almost entirely in his favour as was shown by the petition signed and forwarded to the Government. The facts of this matter are well known to all of you, and my object in writing this letter is to appeal to every member of the Society to see that justice is done to a fellow Jamaican. Are we going to allow ourselves to be dominated and overruled, more especially when we have Right on our side?

The members of the Board of Management occupy their positions through your delegates and their duty is to administer the affairs of the Society so as to provide the greatest possible benefit for the members, and whilst they are naturally entitled to their own opinion in any matter, surely this question has reached a stage where the Board should clearly understand the wishes of the members of the Society which I know are that the injustice which has been metered out to a fellow-countryman should be righted and prompt and effective steps taken in this direction. If members will now do his or her part, in constitutional manner, through your delegates, by raising your voices against this wrong, there can be no doubt as to the success that will result.

I am by no means unmindful of the fact that most of the members of the Board of Management fully understand the position, and are strongly in favour of Mr. Coote but the time has now come when the delegates should show their whole-hearted approval and support of such an attitude, so that the whole Board might be aware that their action in this matter is being watched, not only by members of the Society but by Jamaica as a whole.

In conclusion I would remind you that it is the duty of every man and woman throughout the world to fight Injustice and to right wrongs fearlessly not influenced by personal friendship and or undue pressure. Mr. Coote is no friend of mine; I can therefore write with an open mind. This man has served the Society, in fact the whole island, faithfully and well for many years and he is still fully capable of doing so for years to come. Are we going to stand aside and see him "butchered to make a Roman holiday" and do nothing?

I am etc.,
Alexander Bustamante,
1a Duke Street,
Kingston.

PROTECTING JAMAICA

THE EDITOR,

Sir,

It is my fervent hope that you will publish this letter. I am mystified and alarmed at the articles from your pen in a recent issue of the "Gleaner" one entitled, "No fear" and the other "The Problem".

"We should not fear as America would protect us." Since when have we become American citizens that we should look towards America for protection and what is wrong with Old England? If we were to look towards America for protection we might ask England to turn us over to America. If we understand rightly, England said that her Colonies are not for sale nor should her peoples be bartered away for any consideration.

You casually remarked that you are pleased with the interest exhibited by the people in this country in its safety. There is nothing to be pleased about and it is perfectly natural for one to be concerned for one's own safety. You also comment on the fact that Jamaica is some four thousands miles away from Europe. You forget that during the last war we were menaced by the pressure of enemy submarines, raiders and a considerable German Fleet in waters near to this island and the German submarine "Deutschland" made several trips to the United States and back, that recently the German "Graf Zeppelin" on its way to South America, passed in close proximity to these shores; that it is possible for aeroplane parts to be sent on these vessels, and assembled with the idea of making raids on strategic points. We have it on the authority of no less a person than Sir Ian Hamilton in prognosticating what the next war is likely to be "that on its outbreak there would be a rush by the mechanised enemy forces to seize enemy property for the purpose of establishing enemy bases, and it is there that the war will be decided, and after that they would turn around on the civilian population and lap them up as cats lap up cream."

One hates to imagine that it is possible to be subjected to attacks by sea and air as in these days aeroplanes cover considerable distances namely from Europe to S. Africa, India and Australia and it is perfectly correct for us to be anxious as to the protection we possess against this without recourse to assistance from the United States or any other foreign Power. I do not think the Editor is serious in suggesting that we should be content to remain at the mercy of others for our protection.

Now with regard to "The Problem", he states that it is the public that has to be considered. We agree with him and instead of putting ideas into the heads of those who are seeking to block the erection of the new theatre, backing up the Police in the confessed inability to handle a situation which should not be beyond their ability namely, the regulation of traffic in the area, if he were to consider the public and endeavour to get the consensus of opinion as to whether this new theatre is wanted or not, he would find that they are looking with alarm at the attempt to deprive them of something which they consider they need, and that the public are viewing with interest the actions of certain members of this Corporate Body in this matter involving the taxpayers in heavy costs and endeavouring to put back the hands of the clock. They may find that in the near future, such action may have severe repercussions and that the public is seriously considering whether they are being properly represented by those they select to certain bodies and if the people's interest is as it should be — the first and only consideration.

So often the writing of the Editor is a problem and we can't help viewing it at times with much consideration. This is, of course, very unfortunate for me to depend on him for guiding the people in the right way and if this is not done it becomes more sad than the present Civil War for soon that will end but we cannot see any prospect of that happening to the influence on the public minds and affairs by the Editor's pen.

I hope I am not over pessimistic but I base my opinion on three years of observation. Then those who have the privilege to observe it longer must be about to die in despair.

I am etc.,
Alexander Bustamante,
1a Duke Street,
Kingston,
September 9, 1936.

LLOYD GEORGE'S VISIT

THE EDITOR,

Sir,

I noticed in your impression of today's date you vigorously object to a manifestation which is planned by the people to meet Lloyd George, one of England's greatest men, and perhaps one of the world's greatest, that he is not a Government official and that he is coming here to rest in peace.

I quite agree with the Editor that at present he is not a Government official but the Editor apparently has forgotten that he is still a big public man, and has not yet publicly stated that he has retired from public affairs. I am sure that the members of the Jamaica Imperial Association will certainly not lose the grand opportunity of meeting this well known political figure if not through a public meeting, socially, and so it would seem that whilst the House of Lords (The Jamaica Imperial Association) will have such a great privilege the Editor vigorously objects to the House of Commons (the people) having a similar privilege. However, as I do not intend to lay more stress or weight on the Editor's pen I will conclude by saying that if he thinks he is a dictator as to what the people should or should not do, I personally do not want any dictatorship and whilst we will conform to all reasonable requirements of law and order, the wishes of the people must be given due weight.

I am etc.,
Alexander Bustamante,
1a Duke Street,
Kingston,
October 26, 1936.

SPANISH CIVIL WAR

THE EDITOR,

Sir,

It was with the greatest pleasure and appreciation that I read your editorial of today's date on the true position of the Spanish Civil War.

Knowing as I do how much misleading and mischievous propaganda has been published throughout the world, it is indeed most welcome to read an article such as your own and Captain Dare's of Mandeville with so much in your knowledge of real facts as compared with Mr. Mather's late of the Boler Islands, Spain.

I had intended commenting on Mr. Mather's interview, but he being a stranger within our gates, I thought I would spare him some discomfort. At the same time, I feel he should have learnt the true facts before he attempted to give an interview which is not consistent with the true facts as you, Captain Dare, and I know them.

However, many contradictory statements may be given on any fact, but there can only be one true statement.

I sincerely thank and congratulate you.

I am etc.,
Alexander Bustamante,
1a Duke Street,
Kingston.

WATER METERING

THE EDITOR,

Sir,

With your permission I would like to make a few brief comments on the attitude of the Hon. George Seymour at the "Protest Water Meeting" held at the Ward Theatre.

I am an admirer of courage, and Mr. Seymour certainly gave abundant proof of this quality in facing a hostile audience so frankly where he had erred naturally defending himself where he felt he was harmless, and finally promising his support to the resolution.

If his promised assistance is as sincere as his courage, he will be a tower of strength on our side and I welcome him to our ranks.

I am etc.,
Alexander Bustamante,
1a Duke Street,
Kingston.
Nov. 13, 1936.

THE NEEDLEWORKERS

THE EDITOR,

Sir,

The forgotten needleworkers! They are despondent, they are in despair of the dismal future which will be worse than the cloudy present; unless the Government and the Elected Members enact laws to prevent the wholesale dumping of cheap ready-made dresses in the Island or to inflict such a high tariff that dressmakers can compete.

You will recall that during the administration of the present Governor, His Excellency Sir Edward Denham, a high tariff has been placed on Japanese goods coming to the island to prevent them competing with British manufacturers thus protecting British manufacturers and workers — men and women alike.

From a patriotic point of view for the English this was an excellent move, but with due respect to them, I must say patriotism must first begin at home; and whether these ready-made dresses are imported from England, America or elsewhere, our needleworkers should be given protection for they are weak, they cannot protect themselves. Their men, if any, cannot protect them either for they are in distress and in need owing to the world's economical crises. I am sure that you are aware of the irrefutable fact that many relatives depend upon these needleworkers to help them from complete starvation and nudeness.

I now make a direct appeal to the Governor and Elected Members not to forget these needleworkers who are silently looking to this Government for protection. Their case is a pathetic one; many dozens have been already thrown out of work owing to the wholesale dumping of these ready-made dresses in the island, without any other avenue open for them elsewhere. Hundreds after this Christmas Season will be thrown out of work; the doors will be closed for they will not be able to earn sufficient money even to pay their rent, much more to buy their daily bread. Can anything be more pathetic?

Hundreds of our men, perhaps thousands, have lost hope of regaining themselves from poverty. We cannot and must not allow our needlewomen to suffer from this same condition through lack of protection. Every and all countries today are protecting their workers; therefore, we must not sacrifice our womanhood either through lack of knowing or appreciating the plight of our needleworkers or through wanting to please other nations. Again, I ask the Governor respectfully to use his influence to have protection given to these women.

Elected Members, I cannot see how you will help in this matter, I cannot conceive the belief that you will shrink from your duty; I cannot and will not believe that you have not got some national feeling towards the women of your island. You cannot and you must not shrink from such an important duty. It is imperative that you must act now. You and Government have surged through many Bills that were not urgent; today the needs of the needlewomen are silently pleading with you to do your duty, if not through love, for the sake of humanity.

This matter is not affecting only the Corporate Area, but also affecting needleworkers throughout the island. The dumping of ready-made dresses in the island will cause island-wide crises, it will send many more of the inhabitants to unfortunate institutions, it will cause more babies to be sent to the different hospitals for medical treatment, when in truth and in fact the chief reason will be malnutrition.

Mr. Editor, you have the Press at your command and by an article in your Press by your pen some time ago, I have to believe that your heart is along with the needleworkers of our island. Will you please remember them in your Editorial?

No country is allowing their workers to be destroyed; then why do we in Jamaica allow it? We are on the eve of Christmas; there is no need to write hypocritical things, it is a black one for the majority. A decision in this matter in favour of them would lighten their hearts and would keep the fire of hope burning for the New Year. I plead with those who are in authority to do the right thing by the women of Jamaica, and not to leave these unfortunate girls to drift to where neither you, the officials of this Government, the people's representative of this island or any other honest person or myself like to go.

Now you are duty bound to protect your own people whether you are from across the seas or of this sunny island and have no right to allow our women to go to destruction and to desolation. We trust in God to do lots of things, perhaps all things, but we cannot leave the immediate future of our women just to Him. In God I trust; in the Governor and the Elected Members I look forward for protection for the women of our island by immediate and effective action.

I am etc.,
Alexander Bustamante,
1a Duke Street,
Kingston,
December 9, 1936.

WATER METERING

THE EDITOR,

Sir,

Mr. S. R. Braithwaite complained in your impression of today's date that I contributed a half of a column in your journal attacking him personally and accusing him of lack of courage in the Water Metering issue but I observe that you have generously given Mr. Braithwaite a three-quarter column; then indeed my friend Mr. Braithwaite has no grievance for you have been quite fair to both of us which is proof that you are not taking any side in the matter.

Mr. Braithwaite has seen fit to descend to personalities but I will not descend to that level, because it would be beneath my dignity and so I shall keep myself within the boundary of the main issue and that is, why did Mr.

Braithwaite advocate, in the Ward Theatre, the metering of clubs and schools, and then in his letter of the 28th inst. to Mr. DaCosta state that he was doing everything possible for the reduction of the price of water to the clubs?

Mr. Braithwaite made a ferocious attempt to wiggle himself out of this main issue by endeavouring to make his readers believe that I commented upon this double-fencing in the matter because I had a personal grievance, and so referred his readers to certain correspondence that passed between himself and myself after the Water Meeting at the Ward Theatre on November 12.

I intend asking the courtesy of your Press to publish three letters that passed between Mr. Braithwaite and myself, because my character is an open one; I hide nothing, good or bad, and my letters will prove that there was no personal issue between himself and myself; I was merely defending the rights and privileges I should have had as a representative of certain of the Citizens' Associations for that night. Anyone who has ever read my letters and who has the slightest understanding of character and psychology will readily realise that even if I had a grievance against any person, I am not the kind of person that would keep it in my breast, but quickly find that person and settle the matter then and there, and stand the consequence, for man is supposed to be sufficiently courageous to accept that which he soweth, good or bad, and when Mr. Braithwaite viciously tried to set out a case by making me to appear to the public as being so small and conceited as his letter implies, he still evades the challenge and that is certainly not an act of courage. Of course, by doing that, he may think that his desire to place me before the public in such an unfavourable light will convince his readers but I am confident that those who know me will accept it for what it is worth.

Mr. Braithwaite referred in a very contemptuous way to the "message" which I claim that I have to deliver to the audience that night and also gives the sub-title of May's "Parliamentary Procedure" in full.

As I said at the Ward Theatre meeting, I was the chosen delegate of certain Citizens' Association numbering about two thousand members, many of whom were not present that night, but desired that the meeting should know the feelings of the Association. Surely this was a message, despite Mr. Braithwaite's comment in his letter of today's date — "message, if you please". If he is serious in not regarding this as a message then I forgive him. I'm quite sure that Mr. Braithwaite must be aware that in all meetings of a public nature the proceeding of such meetings is guided along Parliamentary lines; otherwise if this was not the case disorder would reign, and surely I made no error when I referred him to a leading authority in procedure; and so Mr. Braithwaite tries to make a mountain out of a mole-hill. I am sure I can afford to ignore his unworthy references to my prominence in business life in this city. It is only a continuance of the method he has adopted to avoid the clear-cut point which I have brought before the public. This, in my opinion, shows the greatest sign of weakness I have seen in a man who took part in a matter of public interest. Again I say may courage reign though the heavens fall.

I think I am quite right when I state that in addition to the large and wealthy clubs, one of which Mr. Braithwaite states that he is on the Managing Committee, there are several others whose pleasures are enjoyed by the poorer classes, and it is these smaller clubs that would suffer chiefly if the metering system which Mr. Braithwaite advocated were enforced.

I am etc.,
Alexander Bustamante,
1a Duke Street,
Kingston.
December 31, 1936.

WAGE RATES

THE EDITOR,

Sir,

I feel qualified to enter on the discussion of hotel charges in Jamaica and its comparison with other countries, North, South and Central America also the Spanish West Indies. I am a certified dietician and apart from that I took a hotel course at Louis Hotel Training School, Washington D.C. Therefore, I have a knowledge of the cost of preparation of food, and the cost of raw food here, and other places in discussion. I shall now comment on the interview given to one of your reporters and published in yesterday's issue by "prominent English visitor with matured experience of tourist business in almost every corner of the world".

The writer stated that it is foolish and ridiculous to compare rates in Jamaica with those of London. I agree, for it always is foolish to compare things of a small island with that of a large city. Jamaicans make this mistake always, for unless we Jamaicans, inclusive of well-known merchants who never give their identity,compare things in Jamaica with those of London, we are never satisfied. I can't help but feel that it is only to show off not the much we know of London, but the little most of us do know of any big city, and so whilst our visitor is right in regarding the silly comparison of hotel charges here with that of London, he has made a more ridiculous and preposterous comparison with the charges here and that of the Canary Islands, just as well known to me as Spain proper.

Fruits and vegetables in the Canary Islands are one hundred times more in abundance than they are in Jamaica and three hundred per cent cheaper which is vital to hotel life. Foodstuff is so cheap that one can live in the best family for 2/— per day, board, room and wine. Rent is at least four hundred per cent cheaper than in Jamaica; electricity much cheaper, they are not overburdened like us with license and taxation, even water is cheaper, and although they would not dare to pay over there the low wages as we are paid in Jamaica, one of the most alarming news is that four shillings per day is paid to waiters in the Canary Islands. I do not want to hurt the visitor, and so I hesitate to contradict him, for I believe he has merely made a statement believing it to be true.

Wages paid throughout Jamaica are a disgrace and a calamity, but that is the only thing that is cheap here, for whether our visitor knows it or not, living in Jamaica is the highest of all living, in comparison to the wages paid in other countries.

I would like to see the hotel of any standing in Jamaica that could charge 5/— a day as is done in the Canary Islands, and didn't have to close its doors. Mark you, I quite realise that hotel charges in this island should be 20% less and that also goes for a meal of which certain hotels here make a charge of 10/—. But the much that has been said of the high charges here tends to lead one to believe that they could charge 50% less. This is not fair to the hotel keepers nor to the island, because it would create a feeling amongst our strangers that they are really being robbed, therefore, no one should venture to give their opinion regarding hotel charges here except they had delved into the cost of raw food materials, and have an idea as to even how many ounces of food one normal person should be served; and also to have some knowledge of the cost of preparation, the percentage lost in preparing, and after it had been prepared. Anyone who gives his or her opinion without the knowledge mentioned is similar to a feather caught in a cyclone going at one hundred miles an hour.

I venture to say that our first class hotels here pay up to 1/6 per pound for fresh fish, and out of a pound of such fish after it has been prepared only eight ounces are left for consumption. They pay around the same price for choice tenderloin steak, the best fed chickens are bought at a high price; and let me assure you that a chicken weighing four pounds alive, after it has been roasted there is only one pound left for consumption. I could continue mentioning the prices of many things in Jamaica — inclusive of cauliflower — that would make one's hair stand on edge at the high cost of hotel materials here; and if I were to tell you of the low prices of the same raw food materials in the Canary Islands and Spain, you and I might want to go over to enjoy the cheapest life you have ever heard of and to partake of their precious wine that is given free in many hotels and often in places where one person pays ten cents for one meal which in Jamaica you could not buy for 2/—, for the cost of raw food here is too high.

Then the visitor said we should be able to accommodate strangers for £3. per week. Surely he couldn't mean in our best hotels. He continued saying we should build up a large Summer trade as what they have in the Canary Islands as the climates are similar. I am a Jamaican and want to praise my country to the highest, but in spite of the fact that everything is grown in the Canary Islands as is grown in Jamaica, except ackee, as the visitor remarked (he had forgotten to say "Badoo"), the climate of Jamaica in Summer certainly cannot be compared with that dry and somewhat semi-tropical climate of the Canary Islands, and we will therefore never be able to, even for that reason, to build Jamaica almost to that of the Canary Islands.

I venture to say that it costs our first class hotels here 11/— per day for raw material per capita, and 12/– per day overhead expense for each guest, those with private baths and telephone make the average cost more. The reason is a short one, it must help to pay for other seasons of the year, and that is the case with any tourist resort in any part of the world. If one hotel manager in the island would be frank enough to take us in his kitchen and prove to us the high cost of the menu that the few first class hotels here serve, and give us an insight of their overhead expenses, we would wonder why so much fuss is being made over charges in our first class hotels.

I have no interest in hotels here or abroad. I have merely given an opinion on account of the silly comparison which the visitor made between charges here and the Canary Islands. It is absurd and more absurd yet to ask the Government to regulate prices and profit. Soon the Government will have to enact laws to prevent dogs barking and cocks crowing.

I am etc.,
Alexander Bustamante,
1a Duke Street,
Kingston,
Janauary 19, 1937.

TOURIST PRICES

THE EDITOR,

Sir,

Please allow me to comment on a letter written by Mr. Iver of Mandeville and published in your impression of today's date. An English tourist told him that in a hotel in Jamaica he was charged 18/– for a bottle of whisky when it was sold outside for 10/–. It is only a cheap tourist staying at a hotel who buys Rum and Whisky by the bottle, for he knows as well as the hotel keeper that money is only made off spirituous liquor when it is retailed. In spite of the fact that one buys liquor by the bottle one still expects to be served with ice, water etc., which costs money too.

When Mr. Iver comes in contact with better kinds of tourists I would be glad if he would ask their views on this buying of spirits in hotels by the bottle, and if it is the nicest thing to do. Hotel keepers, to keep their guests from buying spirits by the bottle, might charge the full price they would get if the liquor were retailed.

The section of Mr. Iver's letter dealing with the costs of hotels in Jamaica is very vague. If he were to read a letter which was sent to Messrs. Fred L. Myers and Sons from the Virgin Islands which they thoughtfully had published in this morning's impression, he would notice that the three highest prices charged over there were merely 2% less than the three highest charges in Jamaica's few best hotel charges here that they are not half as high as some make it out to be. I was right when I wrote that a mere reduction of 20% in hotel charges would bring them down to normal and reasonable prices.

It is obviously unfair to compare rates which are charged by small private hotels, whether in Kingston or the country or anywhere in the world, with the rates applicable to proper hotels catering to a more wealthy class and rendering far more extensive and efficient service.

Should the keepers of these first class hotels make up their minds to run even at a loss by reducing their rates to those of inferior hotels, soon the better class guests would not patronise them and then all we would have in Jamaica is cheaper class tourists.

In my previous letter I stated that I was not interested in any hotel here or abroad. Again I say I have not been briefed by anyone, but I am actuated by a sense of fair play.

Criticism is good, but only when it is founded on knowledge of the subject which one speaks of. Surely Mr. Iver's letter does not indicate the above.

I am etc.,
Alexander Bustamante,
1a Duke Street,
Kingston,
January 25, 1937.

"THE DAILY GLEANER"

THE EDITOR,

Sir,

I noticed a couple of letters written by correspondents in which they mentioned something about another daily paper, and emphasizing the fact that a weekly paper is more badly needed than another daily. Today I notice a news article in the 'Jamaica Times' regarding these letters in the 'Gleaner' with the question, "Can the Gleaner truthfully say it has always done its duty to the public?"

I wouldn't have entered this matter if your contemporary did not mention two instances (in which it actually praises itself) in having been the first to bring certain matters before the public. No one must blame this paper for "blowing its own trumpet" — and it certainly needs a long big one — but with all the faults of the 'Gleaner', can the 'Times' even pretend that it has served the public as well as the 'Gleaner'? If this is their suggestion, it seems to be bordering on the line of the greatest audacity.

The writer or writers of these news articles wrote that they were the first to publish the crash of an aeroplane, and that the Myrtle Bank Hotel was going to spend thousands of pounds on the improvements of the Hotel and that subsequently the 'Gleaner' published these news items only in different words. I do not like to be personal, but I am tempted to say that this is the most childish thing that I have ever seen written in any newspaper that I have read. I think it would take first prize for childishness. What a great triumph to have published these items before the 'Gleaner'.....I think the writer or writers should be crowned with an iron helmet. I am tempted to go further and so I would like to say that there seems to be a pathological condition somewhere or the other.

Surely in fighting a duel of any kind we should have sufficient courage to do so by attacking fairly, otherwise we cannot expect the respect of the public. The article shows a lack of intelligence and unbalanced sense of fair play. If this weekly newspaper serves the public as well as the 'Gleaner' does, then one could not say that Jamaica does not produce a good weekly newspaper.

I have no personal interest in the Gleaner, but I must admit that it has been serving this country for a very long time. I have had my little quarrels with them, but on the whole it has served me well and though it is believed that the country can stand another daily newspaper, I venture to say that no one paper would serve us better than the 'Gleaner' has been doing, and I doubt if any one Press would be as fair to us as the 'Gleaner' has been.

I do think that too much is being made about the unfairness of the 'Gleaner', and let it be known that it does not matter how many newspapers you may have in a country, there will always be complaints about each one for the public is never satisfied. I do not think it is fair to hammer so old a friend as the 'Gleaner' so much.

It has been my experience that if one is not pleased with the 'Gleaner' one can go the the Editorial Department and receive courtesy, and if one chooses to approach Mr. Michael DeCordova, the Managing Director, his office is wide open to you. I do not want to be misunderstood or to give the impression that I do not think that there should be two newspapers, for I am a believer in competition, but it is a vile thing to start any propaganda against the Gleaner today; just because we expect to have a new daily newspaper.

I have picked up the weekly paper and thrown it away with disgust; there is so little in it to be read; and I say this with every feeling sincerity that God has endowed me with, I marvel that such a newspaper could dare to attack so good a publication as the 'Gleaner'. The greatest of the 'Gleaner' could truthfully say that it is a most modern and up-to-date newspaper. You may have seen a larger paper than the 'Gleaner' but you have never seen a better edited one; neither have I. You may read the 'London Times' or the 'New York Times', two of the leading newspapers of the world, which give you the news of the world and have their own policy, so has the 'Gleaner'.

Of course we must try to compare the excellency of the 'Gleaner' with the weekly paper. The 'Gleaner' has a seasoned Editor and a large trained staff in the Editorial department. This letter is not to make comparison between two papers for that would be silly. It is chiefly to express my opinion of the unfairness of unjustified criticism of the 'Gleaner' as a newspaper, what dissatisfaction may be felt locally as regards their advertising rates in which opinions differ.

However, no matter how many newspapers we would have in this island, it would be the height of ingratitude to condemn and forsake such a long, true and old friend as the 'Gleaner' has been to Jamaica. I am briefed by no one — no one would dare brief me — but I have a conscience which I shall always satisfy first without any fear whatever, irrespective as to whom my opinion or action would hurt, and that's that.

I am etc.,
Alexander Bustamante,
1a Duke Street,
Kingston.
February 20, 1937.

LADY DENHAM

THE EDITOR,

Sir,

Lady Denham with her endless energy is definitely an asset to Jamaica and its people. She has done much good since she has been here. She has that sterling quality which every man should possess — a keen interest in mankind — in humanity; and among the things she should be commended for is her Embroidery Scheme.

It has been said in the Press that a technical instructor should not be imported for this enterprise, because there are Jamaicans here quite capable of undertaking such a task. This might be true. Jamaicans should get the best of everything in their island, no one can deny that fact; yet looking at things from the broad angle, we must not forget that although the bulk of employees in every department, Government or otherwise, should be Jamaicans a little of what we term "strange Blood" acts as the greatest stimulant to our natives, thus benifiting the country. Can anyone who is not absolutely selfish deny this?

I repeat that Lady Denham is an asset to us. She has been expending much energy in constructive work and she has been given much praise and thanks for the genuine interest she has taken in our island.

I am etc.,
Alexander Bustamante,
1a Duke Street,
Kingston.
March 20, 1937.

Mr. VIVIAN DURHAM

THE EDITOR,

Sir,

The Government and other intelligent people who have read Mr. Vivian Durham's letter which appeared in your issue of today, must be shivering from shock to know that Mr. Durham has intimate knowledge of private correspondence of a very serious nature passed between the Governor and the Mayor. But in the absence of contradiction, we must give him credit that he knows the Mayor's reply; knowing that we must wonder how much lower can the office of the K.S.A.C. descend, that is to say, if Mr. Durham did not get his information officially.

We all know that all correspondence between Government and the K.S.A.C. passes through the Town Clerk's office. One hesitates to believe that serious and important communication was given out to persons who hover around the office; therefore, taxpayers should demand an investigation of this matter, and if it were proved that Mr. Durham got this matter unofficially through the office or from some big officials, what other conclusion could we come to than that an important office has fallen into a pit of disgrace and shame. Surely this office could not be a bed of iniquity as to have given out privately and secretly the Mayor's reply to the Governor. Perhaps the Town Clerk, on investigation, might find out how Mr. Durham obtained knowledge of the Mayor's reply according to his statement. One must not blame this self-appointed spokesman or ambassador for having taken the stand he has.

There is a story of a Jewish gentleman who paid a doctor an exorbitant price to diagnose his illness and who paid the druggist the same for his medicine. When he went home he told his wife how liberal he had been; the wife became alarmed and annoyed at his silliness; the old man then exclaimed, "they must live!" He afterwards tasted the medicine and then threw the bottle and medicine away; the poor wife almost fainted and then the old fellow exclaimed, "I too must live!" After all everyone should live, and if Mr. Durham quoted the Mayor's reply to the Governor correctly, that the reason why he did not make a reply was because the complaint would not name certain Councillors against whom he had grave charges, then the kindest thing I can say regarding him in his absence is that his memory should have lived longer for I told him in no uncertain words that I was ready and willing to identify and confront and give a public statement against the Councillors in question; and my letter to the Governor regarding this same matter did not imply that it was between him and me, but was intended for His Excellency to have an investigation definitely in the matter, and I certainly felt and believed that the opportunity would have been embrased with a view to eradicate rascality.

We in Kingston know Mr. Durham that he is not even a messenger at the K.S.A.C., but what about our sisters and brothers throughout Jamaica that may not share our knowledge and may even think Mr. Durham has replied for the Mayor in an official capacity? And now I hasten to suggest to Mr. Durham never to be in such a haste again.

I am etc.,
Alexander Bustamante,
1a Duke Street,
Kingston,
May 10, 1937.

PUBLIC CAREER

THE EDITOR,

Sir,

What would any responsible person in the Corporate Area think of me if I were to keep up correspondence in the daily press with Mr. Durham? This gentleman stated that he has a public career — "a public career", if you please, friends and readers. If someone has brought himself down to a level where it is felt that it was dignified to divulge the Governor's private correspondence of a serious nature to Mr. Durham, surely that does not mean that I should bring myself to that level to make it appear in the Press that this person is worthy of any consideration. One should keep at a certain level and I do not intend spending valuable powder unless I can see upon what I am using it.

One of the very unfortunate things in politics here is that even some of the respectable candidates for election lower their dignity by associating with some persons with "public" and "political careers". So as to get these figures to hunt them votes for election, and sometimes to act as their public mouthpiece. This method of obtaining votes is even a reflection against the other few candidates who want to win their election with honour and dignity, and make up their minds to lose it rather than stooping to have touts and political heirlings to drum votes from them or to act as their mouthpiece, because people generally say all politicians in Jamaica use touts which is absolutely untrue. Again the liberal Jewish gentleman I wrote about a few days ago, who paid an exorbitant price for doctor and medicine reminds me of one fact that everyone must live, and it is but natural to work for the man who pays the most.

I have seen one Corporation election and one Legislative election here, and my heart was washed in sorrow and my nerves trembled to see the kinds of persons some of these candidates use to drum up votes. If public men are to have much respect in this country or regain that which has been lost, then people should cease voting for all those who have political touts to drum votes or to say a word in their favour; it is a staggering disgrace.

Mr. Durham has made one great point in his letter. He wrote *inter alia* there are "some of impeachable integrity who sit around the civic board". Surely we all know that there are many Councillors of irreproachable characters, high intelligence and worthy of being our representative. The latter is the majority; their acts have been so upright, their conscience so clear, they need have nothing to be fearful of. We also know that in every flock there is a bad sheep, but I fear we have too many spotted ones amongst our public men. The chief point I want to make clear is that Mr. Durham, who takes the role of defender of certain public men, has openly admitted in his letter, which appears in your issue of today's date, that "some who sit around the Civic Board are of irreproachable character", thereby admitting that "some" are not. When he makes such an admission then things must be even more serious than what I know of, and so we must give him credit at least for his frankness.

Before I returned to Jamaica, I understand that there was an investigation held regarding some Councillors and that no time was lost in doing this and now I again wonder why no investigation whatsoever was made regarding a complaint to the Mayor some two years ago. This is a very alarming condition, we want to destroy evil, but when the opportunity comes to do so, it is not taken advantage of. It is a staggering condition; it is regrettable and detrimental to good Government. It is a wonder that Mr. Durham has a "public career", but the temperature of the Corporate Area must have arisen today, the hair on the heads of the inhabitants must have stood straight and their teeth on edge to learn of such a silly pronouncement.

I am etc.,
Alexander Bustamante,
1a Duke Street,
Kingston,
May 20, 1937.

CUSTOS AND M.L.C.

THE EDITOR,

Sir,

Please allow me to suggest to a certain Custos and an Elected Member of a certain parish who seem to be very anxious to keep others out of their parish that it would not be a bad thing to revert to the old custom of walling their parish around, erecting gates and draw-bridges as a method of keeping intruders, including labour orators, and members of other parishes out.

May I in conclusion suggest that the command of the guard at the two gates be given to this Custos and Elected Member respectively.

I am etc.,
Alexander Bustamante,
1a Duke Street,
Kingston.
August 19, 1937.

JAMAICANS IN CUBA

THE EDITOR,

Sir,

Jamaicans are a suffering people. In the 'Gleaner' of September 4th, a pathetic letter was written regarding the plight of Jamaicans in Cuba, and how they are being sent to prison for not being able to pay their land tax, and how "Wise Councillor", whom I presume knows nothing about health conditions in Demerara, is anxious to have the unemployed here sent there to develop that country not knowing or realising that their destruction will be completed by malaria, malnutrition, poisonous snakes and perhaps ferocious lions and tigers; or perhaps he does not care so long as the unemployed is got rid of, whilst we have thousands upon thousands of acres of fertile undeveloped lands here. I am interested in Jamaicans not just at election time, but always, so I suggest to every Jamaican not to go to Demerara for there is much more peril there than in Jamaica.

It is marvellous to note the amount of interest that prospective candidates whether for the Kingston and St. Andrew Corporation or the Legislative Council take in the people on the eve of Election in Jamaica. Hyprocrisy and deceit are mixed with the interest and promises of nearly everyone.

I find that on the eve of election many persons are taking sudden interest in the Jamaica Workers and Tradesmen Union, but when they are called upon to advocate publicly the cause, these politicians' answers are "we will help you but we must think of our own position or profession" or whatever vocation they have to make a living from open advice to the Union is not to have anything to do with these spineless people. The leaders of the Union should not use any influence whatsoever with their members to vote for anyone of the candidates who is either afraid or ashamed or has not enough interest to fight for the Union openly.

I know I will create more enemies by writing this letter, but I am obligated to no man in this island and no man's wrath means anything to me, and I do not intend to raise a straw to help anyone to deceive the workers, they are deceived enough - too much. Why is there all this hyprocrisy and deceit? The answer is insufficient honour and not sufficient respect for the welfare, not just for the masses, but for the whole population of the island. We certainly want changes in the Council, but before we make a change, voters should take inventory of the new prospective candidates as to what interest they showed in the public and country before election time and then if their interest warrants votes, it should be given whether there is a personal dislike or otherwise.

Any man can stand on a platform and tell you to vote for him for there should be a change; that should not be enough for intelligent voters. The questions voters should ask are: has he ever taken any interest in the past? what are his objects for wanting to be elected? is he a sound businessman? And the question I would ask is, why are certain politicians showing such sudden interest behind the screen in the Labour Union?

I am etc.,
Alexander Bustamante,
1a Duke Street,
Kingston.
September 6, 1937.

JAMAICAN'S LABOUR PARTY

THE EDITOR,

Sir,

As special adviser and treasurer of the Jamaica Workers and Tradesmen Union, I would like you to permit me the courtesy of announcing through your columns that the Jamaican's Labour Party is in no way connected to our Union (The Jamaican Workers and Tradesmen Union) and that at no time were any of our officers "taken for a ride" in any Police car to the Criminal Investigation Department. I make this announcement not as a reflection against the Labour Party, for I know nothing good or bad about it, but as the two names are so similar one might be mistaken for the other.

I enclose herein a copy of the letter which was written and sent to Mr. C. Beckford, Secretary of the Jamaican's Labour Party giving the reasons why I could not speak at his political meeting held at 40 Laws Street on September 9th. I take this precaution because my name was published on pamphlets that I would be one of these speakers.

I am etc.,
Alexander Bustamante,
1a Duke Street,
Kingston,
September 13, 1937.

THE LETTER

C. Beckford, Esq.,
Secretary,
Jamaican's Labour Party,
99, King Street,
Kingston.

Dear Sir,

I want to thank you sincerely for having invited me to speak at 40 Laws Street tonight for if you did not think something good of me you would not have taken the trouble to extend to me an invitation; however, I am begging you not to be too hard in your judgement against me because I have now decided not to give an address. I have never made it a policy to make anything but legitimate excuses and so I am going to be frank with you. I am not against the candidates neither am I for them. Why? Because I have never noticed any of them taking any visible interest in public affairs before election time, therefore, I have no good reason to speak there tonight.

I do not quite understand the policy in Jamaica of just presenting one's self to represent the public without having shown any visible interest before. Mark you, I am not saying ill against any of the candidates that have been invited there tonight. I intend to remain neutral. I could have written you a different letter, but I do not intend entering the army of deceit and hyprocrisy that exists in the land of my birth, and I do not intend to say one word to influence labour for or against any candidate unless I have knowledge that warrants one to do so. As you know, I am organizing labour and I must not do anything to influence them except through the dictates of an honest conscience. They have been so much deceived in the past that sometimes I could weep for them, and these words are dictated through a heart so full of love for the unfortunate ones and not from the lips of hyprocrisy.

This letter is not to be considered private, you may use it as you see fit. I hope you will forgive me for not coming, and as a man who I think has travelled, I also hope that you will respect my frankness and will not condemn me too much for my decision in this matter.

Yours faithfully,
Alexander Bustamante.

WORKING FOR THE WORKERS

THE EDITOR ,

Sir,

Your "Meddler" possesses an extraordinary unbalanced sense of justice. He is filled with prejudice against the workers of this island. Had it not been for some good Samaritan who criticised the "Meddler" in this morning's paper under the nom de plume, "Truth", of his statement that "Men who have so much time and money to spare in using their freedom of speech as a license to stir up unrest amongst the workers, they are more of a pest to the banana industry than the borer and ought to be as ruthlessly exterminated", I would not have known of "Meddler's" impudent statement. I am one of the persons that "Meddler" means, because I am helping to organize labour, and am the only one who is using my own money to do so, which "Meddler" terms as stirring up unrest.

Many duels have been fought, much blood has been shed through less impertinence than is in the Press, and it is very fortunate for "Meddler" that duels are prohibited under the British Law, for nothing would give me greater pleasure than to challenge this gentleman whoever he may be, even though I may get the worst of it. The statement of "Meddler" cannot be justly settled through newspaper, it is too serious for that. Unfortunately, "Meddler" is only a nom de plume, his identity is not known, that makes the attack more cowardly.

Mr. Editor, may I suggest to "Meddler" to designate himself as the exterminator of all those who are using their money and time as a license to stir up unrest amongst the workers? I am quite willing to be his subject, so that he might use whatever method he thinks best. No honest person, no one with the slightest sense of justice, fairplay and self respect would have stooped to such a low way of thinking, bordering on the line of imbecility, overstepping the boundaries of civility. No one but a coward would do that. I am glad that my mind lives in a different environment than "Meddler's", and as words cannot settle this affair, as it is not a moral thing to want to exterminate human beings, I will not suggest that "Meddler" should be exterminated, but if I had to suggest that he should be, I would say that a tin of "Black Flag" would be quite sufficient for the job. That is a very effective treatment for all kinds of pests and the cost is not much.

No insult whatsoever from whatever source it may come will ever act as a wet blanket to prevent me using my money and my time to organize the workers of Jamaica, in fact, the more opposition I meet, the more fervently shall I fight. I am called a communist by a certain section. My aims and views are to obtain higher scale of wages, shorter hours, overtime after seven hours of work, more humane treatment, more respect amongst the workers themselves that they should hate no one for their colour or otherwise, that they should be orderly and disciplined, that Government should enact Minimum Wage Law, Workman's Compensation Act, Old Age Pension, that the churches should stand unmolested, and that the unemployed should get work. If these aims and views are communistic, then I am an out and out Red.

I am etc.,
Alexander Bustamante,
1a Duke Street,
Kingston.
September 24, 1937.

A WORD TO "UNIONISTS"

THE EDITOR,

Sir,

Please allow me to explain the objects of Labour Unions to the workers of this island, as the majority does not seem to know.

The objects of Unions are: to get the people to unite in masses to contribute their little money for cases of emergency so that in the time of this and the time of that, the Union will have money to work for the interest of the members the way the Executive Committee thinks best; that there should be labour representatives who will represent the cause of labour not alone to their employers but to Government; to work for better understanding between Labour and Capital; to work for better wages, better working conditions, and to work in the interest of the unemployed to seek ways and means to obtain them work.

A labour union is nothing more than the working people's club where they can unite for one common good, for one common cause, so that they can bring their grievances to their officers. Union members, if you want to be successful you must remember that you must follow your officers and must not expect them to follow you, and for that reason the officers should be men of intelligence, honesty and reliability. You, the workers are seeking justice from your employers, then to accomplish this you must also measure out justice and fairplay to them, however, cruel they may be.

You must never attempt to strike against them without first bringing to their notice, through the right channel, that you are dissatisfied, and even when capitalists may refuse to do anything, it is your duty to persist in an amicable way to gain your ends before you resort to strikes. Strikes must be the last thing on your minds, they must only come about — if they have to come — after we have exhausted every arbitrary method with capitalists and Government and both turn their backs on us; then and only then it is time for us to make up our minds not alone to starve for one common cause, but if needs be to die for it with a smile upon our quivering lips. I do not agree with these strikes that have been going on here and there; it might help a little section, but it will prevent progress of the Union, and I want the workers to know that if they want my help they will have to follow my advice, I do not intend following theirs.

If I had taken interest in the Union because I expect a salary from it, in order to get it I no doubt would follow the members of the Union, but I have never seen one penny of the Union's money; I don't want any; it costs me my own to travel around the island to do Union work in Kingston, not Russia's as some loudmouth, evil-minded people have written and said, and although my heart is for all classes of labour, I have my prestige to protect.

I repeat that these little strikes throughout the island must be stopped; we were not all born to be leaders otherwise we would need no clubs nor Unions. Workers of all kinds join the Jamaica Workers and Tradesmen Union, make it the biggest thing in the history of Jamaica. I know you have reasons to strike, but this is the wrong way to obtain success, more so at this present time. I now request and direct all Unionists in this island who are on strike to return immediately to their respective occupations and send to Union headquarters their grievances which I know are many. How can you expect to live in a house before first making a roof?

I am etc.,
Alexander Bustamante,
1a Duke Street,
Kingston.
November 4, 1937.

ERECTION OF STABLES AT KNUTSFORD PARK

THE EDITOR,

Sir,

I hold no brief for Knutsford Park Limited, as far as I can remember I have never spoken to Mr. Audley Morais, but I am very pleased that His Worship the Mayor, Councillors Penso, McLaughlin, Duval and Barton did not agree to the prosecution of the Company for the violation of the Municipal Building Regulations by the erection of certain stables for the accommodation of the ponies of the polo team to visit Jamaica shortly.

It has been acknowledged by Knutsford Park Limited that they have infringed upon the law; it is of course decidedly wrong, but it is human to err. Therefore, I think we should be merciful to those who recognise their errors, more so when an apology has been given as has been the case in this matter by Mr. Morais on behalf of his Company.

At the same time I do not write this letter with any feeling of condemnation against those Councillors who insisted on prosecution, as it might have been only over-zealousness in upholding the Law; but I think we need a little more of that spirit of give and take in this island. The extremity should only be used when there is no other alternative.

I am etc.,
Alexander Bustamante,
1a Duke Street,
Kingston,
January 12, 1938.

RADIO BALLYHOO

THE EDITOR,

Sir,

I imagine you have been reading some references to ancient history in a certain newspaper some days ago that St. Paul was rude at times, and Martin Luther was noted for his rudeness etc. Let us not forget that in those days even the ass spoke to Balaam when he was being smitten.

I do not want to smite Mr. Jas. L. Sawers, J.P., for whom a letter was published in your daily contemporary of even date, but I would like to speak to him through your press and instruct him a little regarding fellowship and unselfishness.

As I have already said, all I intend to do, regarding Radio Ballyhoo, I do not intend writing anymore letters on this subject, more so to reply to anonymous writers, and so I shall only select the following words of Mr. Sawers' letter. "I see no reason for anyone trying to defend others who are quite capable of defending themselves." Mr. Editor, the lack of fellowship and overwhelming trait of selfishness that live amongst so many of us

Jamaicans are two of the things which I have been exhausting myself upon through your press. Could there be anymore selfishness and lack of fellowship than those which Mr. Sawers had demonstrated in the above quoted words? Is it possible that while age goes forward, wisdom, unselfishness and fellowship go backward, or sideways like the crab? When one stops to think those words are the thoughts and feeling of a J.P., one wonders if such a person upon whom honour has been bestowed could set a better example. Doesn't this gentleman know enough to realise that one defends another, whether he is capable of defending himself or not? It is not chiefly the person he is defending, but the desire to defend justice and fair play, which desire is actuated by that feeling of fellowship to mankind, which is apparently lacking in Mr. Sawers.

Surely, when the younger people read this kind of nonsense in the Press, they are likely to follow it as good example of manhood, more so when it comes from a person whose power of thinking and whose understanding should be better and who should consider more or better before he makes uncivilized remarks in the Press, for it is certainly not civilization to think so narrowly.

Did America enter the Great War because she sincerely believed that England, France and her other Allies would have been whipped or was she actuated chiefly by a feeling of fair play and justice? Whilst the war would have lasted longer if she had not gone, surely there is not one of us Britishers who believe that the Allies would have lost without the help of America, although we must admit that America did help materially and that without her aid conquest would have been more difficult for the Allies and so no one sees that even nations will go to the help of greater nations chiefly to demonstrate their sense of justice.

In Jamaica nearly everyone is just looking out for himself; a man's enemy can do no good, his friend can do no harm, and the press is generally used not to express opinions according to their feeling regarding the circumstances, and then comes to a manly and just decision; but they inject their personal feelings whether it consists of grudge or friendship.

Civilization has not done as much for us as it was expected to do, otherwise the heart of justice would not be almost dead, fellowship almost unknown, with wisdom lagging behind, whilst age increases.

May the younger generation be less sprinkled with this kind of breed who reads and does not understand well; may they not suffer from the overwhelming traits of selfishness, hyprocrisy, narrow-mindedness and envy. Only when these ills are felt and less pronounced among us will we be able to say that civilization has a real and true purpose.

May this letter serve a useful purpose for Mr. Sawers and others who think in the same avenue; may he never forget that before one rushes into public print, one must think and do so thoroughly, otherwise one may have regrets.

I am etc.,
Alexander Bustamante,
1a Duke Street,
Kingston.
March 9, 1939.

RADIO BALLYHOO

THE EDITOR,

Sir,

Please allow me to further instruct Mr. Jas. L. Sawers of Enfield not on fellowship or selfishness, but on the control of one's mind before writing to the press.

Mr. Sawers' letter which appeared in your issue of today's date in reply to one I wrote in your journal somedays ago, is a most violent one. Of course, the newspaper violence is not better than the physical; either is bad.

May I say to Mr. Sawers that in order to have control over one's mentality when one is provoked, it is necessary first to control violent feelings so as to control the nerves of one's body in order that the mind may be rational. If Mr. Sawers had used these efforts it is my belief that his letters would not have been so violent, and would have been more comprehensive. Please Mr. Sawers, I suggest that you do not attempt to write another when you are somewhat annoyed, without counting ten.

Mr. Sawers penned an inter alia, that when he wrote in another Press he was only defending the honour of his country. Gee! I love the word honour, it fascinates me, and nothing would please me more than to see correspondents imitate Mr. Sawers by writing more of honour, but he was defending "Radio Ballyhoo". I therefore, cannot see when the honour of his and my country was involved or affected. To my mind it's merely a frivolous word.

The honour of this nor no other country was involved neither did the ass speak to Balaam in the time of Martin Luther or St. Paul; I merely wanted to convey to my readers that the days gone by were different from today, and the proof is that the inferior ass of today does not speak.

Whilst envy and selfishness overrule civilization, one is often envied for the superior mentality with which one has been endowed, and some of us mistake this superior mentality for greed or monopoly or love of human applause.

Mr. Sawers further penned, "America entered the war to save herself; her ships were being sunk, American lives were lost, besides what would become of her if the Allies had lost?" This statement of Sawers does not possess one word of justice and fair play, but it is highly tainted with ingratitude. We are cursed in Jamaica with that trait. We even kick our friends just to welcome a newcomer. I would like to instruct Mr. Sawers, but again it might fall on stony ground.

It is quite reasonable to think America also thought of her own destiny when she entered the Great War, yet I feel sure that Mr. Sawers' statement regarding this great country would not be received in the British Commonwealth with popularity. The good she has done in joining the Allies will long live in the minds of the Allies' family and will no doubt be handed down by posterity.

I doubt if any greater ingratitude could come from a pen than that of Mr. Sawers. Lest it be forgotten, America had the privilege to have joined with Germany if she wanted to, and even though it would have been more difficult for her to have transported her troops to the Rhineland, it could have been done. I could not condone the ingratitude that has been penned by

Mr. Sawers with my silence, thus the chief reason why I replied as the major portion of this letter is worthy of serious consideration.

I am etc.,
Alexander Bustamante,
1a Duke Street,
Kingston.
March 21, 1938.

PS. If America had not entered the war she would have been just where she is today as according to her geography she is not subject to tidal waves or volcanic eruptions.

Rev. J.T. DILLON

THE EDITOR

Sir,

On or about November 1st, last year, you published a letter from the Rev. J. T. Dillon of Balaclava against the dreadful economical conditions of this island etc. In your issue of today's date, you published another letter from the same Rev. Gentleman in which he attacked me because I reported similar conditions in England; he even went so far as to ask, "Are we going to sit still in this the Centenary Year of Emancipation, and someone whom we do not know to give out to the world that conditions among us are but little removed from those existing among savages?" Just imagine that an obscure minister should have the temerity to have made such remarks, but after many readers shall have read the Minister's letter of about November 1st., and that of today, I feel sure that he will be like a king without a throne.

I am going to make it my point of duty to hold a public meeting at Balaclava so as to give the public a chance to testify against my friend.

Please be good enough to have both Mr. Dillon's letters reproduced, thereby preventing my replying to him "in extenso", whilst I beg to refer my readers to Mr. Dillon's attack on me of even date.

I am etc.,
Alexander Bustamante,
1a Duke Street,
Kingston.
April 29, 1938.

LABOUR LEADERS

THE EDITOR,

Sir,

My friend the "Speaker" wrote in his article to your issue of even date "Some persons in Jamaica, I refer especially to those who claim to be labour leaders, have certainly overstepped the bound of propriety".

As war is declared all around on reading his utterances, I decided then and there to declare war upon him, but on reflection, felt it would serve no useful purpose as my friend is like an extinct volcano.

I am etc.,
Alexander Bustamante,
1a Duke Street,
Kingston.
May 10, 1938.

BUSTAMANTE UNION

THE EDITOR,

Sir,

Ever since I returned to my native land, I have been taking outstanding interest in all classes of workers. During this time, scores of people of different classes, inclusive of the wealthy, endeavoured to discourage my activities; still I continued and intend to do so in some way or another as long as life lasts, but it is a known fact that in Jamaica some of the same people whom one tries to help out of poverty are the very ones in whose hearts lives a feeling of jealousy. As a matter of fact, in Jamaica, whenever one makes success for himself or the good of the people, that is sufficient to arouse jealousy against that individual or group of people.

I noticed in the press where Mr. Chisholm, a political failure, has been attacking me, but being so very busy I refuse to waste my time on him. Mr. Chisholm's attack can only be due to one thing, — that is the Omnibus workers' refusal to associate with his union, known as the Chauffeur's Union, if there is such a Union, as they quite realise that it cannot help them in any way or form.

I have also observed two letters in your Press in which it was stated that the Unions should not be called Bustamante Unions. My name is not upon the Unions because I want to advertise it or I want glory; for it is a known fact that my name is an international one known throughout the civilized world, but jealousy will creep in here and there in the breasts of the narrow-minded. It is not glory I want; it is results for all classes of workers, and there are many proofs that I have been obtaining results little by little. The suggestion of putting my name to the Union came from Mr. Ross Livingstone who strongly suggested that it should be done for different reasons, chiefly to prevent people with little petty and questionable societies extracting monies from unfortunate people by saying that I was along with them.

If I were to follow these petty writers one would throw the sponge in the air and give up the field of labour, but that would be a sad thing to hurt the interest of some thousands of people, through a few possessing irresponsible minds who are only capable of endeavouring to disrupt the interests of their brothers and sisters.

When one attempts to better the conditions of one's people, one must expect to put up with impertinence for there has never been a man who has tried to better the conditions of his country who has not been abused and sometimes persecuted, but love of one's people should overcome all persecution even the penalty of death. Still it is quite time that the minority, who are always ready to disrupt the interests of the people, stop for one moment and think of their uselessness in this stony world. As it is now, tens of thousands of members have been clamouring that my name should appear on the Union button and if it does go there, it will be entirely against my desire and my will, for again it will be said that my name should not be upon the Union button.

I wish one of these people who have been writing these things will be bold enough to come forward right away and start Unions of their own in competition with those I have started, to prove their courage and to prove their intelligence, as I am one of those persons who fear no competition whatsoever. The work of these Unions is being carried on by merit; by courageous, intelligent and patriotic people, and so occupied are we in the interest of the people that we will have no more time to reply to narrow-minded and jealous people in a world which there is not even room for them.

I am etc.,
Alexander Bustamante,
1a Duke Street,
Kingston.
August 23, 1938.

THE EDITOR,

Sir,

Your editorial entitled "Ballyhoo" is very comical, and I take this opportunity to extend to you a feeling of welcome which unfortunately is intermingled with a feeling of dissappointment regarding your bad taste of this editorial.

It is my considered opinion that you should at least make an attempt to prove to us your worth, and Mr. Editor, before attacking the two gentlemen, Messrs. Michael DeCordova and Lewis Ashenheim, who might not have done as much as they could for this island, but at least tried to do something more than once.

I think your remarks concerning these two gentlemen in connection with the offer they made to Government to erect a broadcasting station in Jamaica which has been turned down by Government is most unkind and it seems to me that your only intention was to smear your pen with injustice. Why?

I read the interview in the "Daily Gleaner" given by Mr. DeCordova and at no time did he ever suggest that their suggestion to Government was made through a philanthropic spirit but merely because they thought that such an undertaking would be of benefit to the country, to themselves and to the shareholders. No one in Jamaica is so rich as to promote commercial understanding just for philanthropic reasons, whether it is in the newspaper world or otherwise and I cannot see any harm in Government granting permission to any group of individuals to establish such a station because Government has the power to check any unconstitutional propaganda and also has the power to take it over in time of war if need be. While Government broadcasting station by Government would be worse for the inhabitants, because there is not the slightest doubt that Government would control public opinion more than a private concern would. No man in this country has shown more courage than I have to speak out fearlessly and frankly, but before one speaks, one must think first of justice and fair play, otherwise, he may appear ridiculous in the sight of unintelligent people of varied temperaments.

I hold no brief for Mr. DeCordova or Mr. Ashenheim or anyone else in Jamaica; I am obligated to no one nor the Government but I could not condone your bad taste — your injustice to these two men with my silence thus this letter, Mr. Editor.

In this your said Editorial you wrote that it is the ordinary Jamaican listener who matters — it is he who will have to pay for the dubious privilege of a local broadcasting station.. While I appreciate the fact that it is the ordinary people that pay always, it appears to me that you are playing the fiddle and the harp at the same time — that you have tried to make us believe that you are thinking of the interest of the ordinary Jamaican — that they mean much to you. I could not help smiling because on the first column of your front page of your first issue you wrote "Congratulations come from distinguished people." Does that mean that the only congratulations to your Press that are worthy are those that come from those whom are termed distinguished from who is not? Isn't it the ordinary Jamaican who will help to make your paper a success then why all this "ballyhoo" of congratulations from distinguished people. This reminds me of an English Lord — a distinguished visitor who came to our shores a short time ago and who turned out to be a distinguished hotel brawler. We have too much of this sort of thing heretofore so much that I feel that the ordinary people of Jamaica have got fed up with same, inclusive of myself.

If you are not a stranger to our shores I might have smeared my pen with blood but not with that of barricades as you penned. May I suggest to you Mr. Editor a little more justice, a little more fair play and a little more caution in your writing so that you may win the respect of your people of this Island as an Editor. You owe your paper, which I welcome, that much duty. May I further suggest that it would be well and wise at least for the present for you to associate yourself with people who will always be ready and willing to dare you when you attempt to tackle problems which need more knowledge of local temperaments and needs. As a kind word of advice, this would serve you a good purpose and doing so you may be able to carry out the destiny and happiness of your Press.

In conclusion, the writer being something of a revolutionist, hopes that you will not debar this letter from your Press. Of course, he is not writing in ragged garb or smeared with blood of barricades nor is he distinguished in a morning coat, but passes pleasant manners and is a businessman.

Thanking you for your early publication.

I am etc.,
Alexander Bustamante,
1a Duke Street,
Kingston.

Footnote:

Mr. Bustamante is more wordy in his letter than was the original article at which he protests. Still his letter is given in full for reasons which will be obvious to discerning readers. But it is strange to find a self-confessed revolutionist ready to support an obvious monopoly. Maybe it is because he is indeed a businessman. — Editor.

THE JAMAICA STANDARD

THE EDITOR,

Sir,

May I have the privilege of commenting on your footnote regarding my letter of protest concerning "Radio Ballyhoo", which letter appeared in your newspaper on Tuesday?

The best way for peace Mr. Editor, is silence, but being so much of a revolutionary I cannot adopt this method, therefore, I am always ready to throw my gauntlet at the feet of anyone. I can readily see that you are the veteran tactician, and that when you are concerned you will use any and every method to extricate yourself and so you wrote, inter alia, "Still his letter is given in full for reasons which will be obvious to discerning readers." I do believe that when you wrote these words your mind was almost blank, therefore you could not have meant much, and instead of seeking the opinion of a pathologist, I sought that of legal minds and was advised that your defence was unworthy of consideration.

"It is strange to find a self-confessed revolutionist ready to support an obvious monopoly". To that I agree, but would say that in a country like Jamaica which I feel sure could not support more than one broadcasting station could then be termed monopolistic, irrespective of whom the promoters may be. No. Mr. Editor, I am appealing to you to be fair, I am glad to have your paper and I hope that one day we will become better friends, you and I, but a little more justice and fair play from your pen would act as a magnet to draw me nearer to you; then and only then could we be better friends.

I am etc.,
Alexander Bustamante,
1a Duke Street,
Kingston,

Footnote:

This column is becoming Mr. Bustamante's own at the expense of other readers who wish to voice opinions. I therefore suggest that Mr. Bustamante dines with me and we can further continue these affectionate personalities which I feel no longer interest our many readers. — Editor.

THE JAMAICA STANDARD

THE EDITOR,

Sir,

Having extended to me a suggestion in your footnote of my letter appearing in your Press of today's date, it would be considered impolite if I did not reply. No, Mr. Editor, I must politely refuse to accept your invitation to dine with you. How do I know if I would not have to pay for the numerous delicacies that you would surely order for yourself if I had accepted your invitation. I would not mind that so much, but you might repeat your order. You see, Mr. Editor, I have been a globe trotter myself and I am quite accustomed to those little games and so I shall keep very far from you.

Rudeness appears to be your outstanding asset as an Editor, and you have given me further proof that you would not hesitate to resort to the most ungracious and undignified method to extricate yourself from an uncomfortable position. With more wisdom you would have less need for unbecoming journalistic tactics. If you do not want continuous correspondence in your Press you should not have attacked Messrs. Michael DeCordova and Lewis Ashenheim unjustly, and as long as you think that attacking personalities without justification is the best method to bring your Press into prominence, you will be repeatedly attacked in your Press and if you should prove yourself cowardly enough to suspend these attacks from correspondents who possess some sense of justice and fair play, it will be done through other newspapers, or even by pamphlets on the streets — and that's that.

It does not matter to me whether you want to publish this or any other letter from me.

I am etc.,
Alexander Bustamante,
1a Duke Street,
Kingston.

Footnote:

Then why write? If Messrs. Michael DeCordova and Lewis Ashenheim consider they have been attacked unjustly, we will generously afford them the same publicity in our columns as given to Mr. Bustamante. Meantime, my invitation to dinner still stands — and I would not have made it if I did not intend to pay. — Editor.

JAMAICA STANDARD: BROADCAST BALLYHOO

THE EDITOR,

Sir,

I owe you a basketful of thanks for being fair enough to publish my letter which appeared in your Press of today's date protesting in the name of justice and fair play against your remarks concerning Messrs. Ashenheim and DeCordova with regards to their request or suggestion to Government to allow them to promote and establish a broadcasting station in Jamaica.

I want you to realise one thing, of course, and that is, although I do wish the "Gleaner" continued success, in my heart of hearts I desire that your Press be blessed with further success, and that your stay in our island will be an enjoyable one, accompanied with good health.

May I be allowed to mention that in the second to the last paragraph of my letter which appeared in today's issue, the copy of my letter shows that the third word is "were" and not "are" as appears in the Press.

Good luck and good health.

I remain,
Yours faithfully,
Alexander Bustamante.

IN DEFENCE OF MONEY-LENDERS

THE EDITOR,

Sir,

In your issue of today's date in concluding your leader "Poverty in Jamaica" you stated that the cause of poverty and distress prevalent in Jamaica is due to the existence of the moneylender and invited me to suggest a remedy "to rid ourselves of the incubus".

It is a matter of further dissappointment and greater surprise to me to find that a paper from which we the public hope so much should continue to fall into the error of bad logic.

It must be patent to any average thinker that since money-lending only flourishes in consequence of the lack of means in a country (as for instance throughout India today) it is childish to assume that the ills suffered by the community are directly attributable to the money-lender, and that to do away with him will bring the millennium with everybody happy and prosperous. Do you realise that many a man and woman in this community has been forced to go to the money-lender to raise the means to save him or herself from being sold out or imprisoned for failing to be sufficiently "tax-minded" and to have the money (even if they have no food) to satisfy the demands of the Tax Bailiff? No, Mr. Editor, the poverty and distress now rampant in the country will not be relieved that way.

Do you know that without the money-lenders, the dead of plenty would have to be buried as paupers, and that many more would have to be sent to prison for all kinds of fines?

The existing mass of poverty, hunger and raggedness amongst the middle and labouring classes is not a thing of over night growth, but is worse today owing to a callous Government, ill advices, and many Elected Members whose mentality and knowledge do not entitle them to be our representatives. Up to about twenty years ago, although there was poverty and some employment, these conditions were not so acute. Since then, everything has tended to accentuate them, higher cost of living, increase of population and no outlet, exclusion from good agricultural lands (I understand) previously obtainable from the big landlords at low rental, rapid increase of taxation, trade licence etc., hardly any increase of wages, increase of inferiority of quality of imported goods, coupled with severe increase of prices, decrease in the ability and interest of administrators and representatives, and capping all, increasing steadily year after year, more and yet more spending – wasteful spending – of public's money, spending not based on the increase of saleable produce by the agricultural population of the island, but spending for the sake of satisfying personal and political ambitions.

The remedy? What is the use of suggesting? Will anything be done by those in authority in Jamaica, and by others who can help? I fear not. The remedy for some of the ills are:– That our people be sent back to the lands – real good lands, and be given some money to make a fair start which the Government would collect over a long period of years.

That local industries be established, I should say increased, for everyone of us is not suitable for agriculture, and if everyone were sent back to the lands, there would be no one to purchase the products.

That there should be a Minimum Wage Law is questionable.

Have you ever stopped to think of the wages — of the terrible low wages that is being paid in our most prominent street of Kingston to the store girls and boys? Do you know that there is a certain store in King Street that pays as low as nine shillings per week to their shop assistants? These people whilst working must borrow money or starve, and finally they must go in bankruptcy, for even without interest sometimes for sympathy's sake, they cannot repay and must finally resort to bankruptcy.

Much has been said about money-sharks, and whilst I agree there are unscrupulous money-lenders, all the latter are not in the same category, but are these money-lenders who charge over 100 per cent of monies which are very often never returned to them, worse than the dry goods store that make a profit from 100 to 250 per cent? Are they as much danger to the community as the shark who pays his shop girls in King Street as low as nine shillings per week, and his cashier fifteen shillings? Ah, Mr. Editor, you are a green horn here. The ills of the country are more grievous than what you can imagine. Are you in a position to write about these employer sharks when some of them are the shareholders of your Press? Many of the stores in King Street are bad, but there is one that if the girls were to give you an interview regarding their salary, it would be a revelation that would upset your stomach. The price that is paid for labour throughout this country with some exceptions of course, is nauseating.

Please get at the roots of the evils that have brought us so much hunger and raggedness, and not at imaginary ills, for that is the only way you can prove to the suffering people of this country that you are sincere, otherwise everyone will realise that your only desire is to be personal, and will further realise that your knowledge of journalism is very much more peculiar than the knowledge of the writer, of business. These little peculiar sensations that you would like to create will only rebound and break your glass window which you have exhibited so prominently since your very first editorial — your bad taste.

If money-lending should be stopped what would become of certain Elected Members when they rank amongst some of the greatest money borrowers of Jamaica?

If you will allow I will return to the subject.

I am etc.,
Alexander Bustamante,
1a Duke Street,
Kingston.

Footnote:

Nobody suggested the millennium would come with the removal of the money-lender. But it would certainly be a step in the right direction. From its beginning "The Standard" has argued for higher wages, for the establishment of local industries, for small-holdings and better housing. It will continue to advocate such policies. And if our desire to remove abuses necessitates dealing with personalities and is considered bad taste, we shall continue with bad taste. Mr. Bustamante himself in his recent speech at the Parade dealt entirely with personalities — The Governor of Jamaica, the Elected Members and the Editor of "The Standard". Bad taste is apparently in the air. — Editor.

THE AUTHOR

Frank Hill, C.D., was born in St. Andrew, Jamaica, on November 25, 1910 *(the Coronation Year of King George V)* and saw the passing of four British Monarchs. He shared a glass of gin-and-tonic with the reigning Queen of Jamaica at a Press Reception at King's House in April 1975. Trade Unionist, political analyst, historical researcher, broadcaster, public bureaucrat in charge of Jamaican culture for the decade since Independence, Hill has been publicly recognised for his distinguished career by the Government of Jamaica. He was awarded the Gold Musgrave Medal for Literature and made the Commander of the Order of Distinction for public services.